MW00790318

THE TWO JERUSALEMS

MATTHEW WISEMAN

The Two Jerusalems

My Conversion from the Messianic Movement to the Catholic Church

IGNATIUS PRESS SAN FRANCISCO

Cover:
Matthew Wiseman and his father
praying at the Kotel in Jerusalem
(Western Wall, proximate to the Temple Mount)
Cover based on a personal photograph provided by the author,
aided by same, but higher resolution, detail of the Kotel,
Adobe Stock Images/Lucia Pitter

Cover design and graphic photo editing by Enrique J. Aguilar

ISBN 978-1-62164-724-9 (PB)
ISBN 978-1-64229-320-3 (eBook)
Library of Congress Control Number 2024938145
Printed in the United States of America ♾

To my parents, who never stopped
teaching me their love of Jesus.

"My son, keep thy father's commandment,
and forsake not the law of thy mother."
(Prov 6:20, KJV)

CONTENTS

Part I

Midland (1989–2002)

I

My mother's people, among whom I was mostly raised, are old Southerners, largely Appalachian until they immigrated to Texas in the waning decades of the nineteenth century. The Trents, her mother's family, were largely respectable people of Anglo-Saxon Protestant stock who entered Virginia early in the 1600s. They worked hard to get by and only sometimes prospered—until the business acumen of my great-grandfather brought them into the middle class for the next three generations. Her father's family was different. The Davidsons left Scotland in disgrace after fighting for Bonnie Prince Charlie in the uprising of 1745, though the clan was conveniently delayed on the way to Culloden and did not actually participate in the battle.[1] They fled to the New World to make a fresh start, but their history is clouded by family silence about rapscallions and misdeeds. My mother once asked my great-grandmother, "Tell me about the time the Davidson boys all got in a fight", to which my great-grandmother replied, "Which time?" My mother pressed her, "The time they got out the guns and were shooting at each other", but my great-grandmother stalwartly maintained, "Which time?" And that was the end of that. They were true Highlanders, often outlaws—a romantic and tragic story. Both branches

[1] The identification of the Davidson family with the Highland Clan Davidson is conjecture on my part, as there is another Davidson clan and the history of the Davidson family is obscure.

made their way from Virginia to Tennessee and then out to West Texas.

My father's family has an oddly similar tale. His mother's family, the Esteses, were dyed-in-the-wool Methodists, respectable people with their roots in county Kent, in the respectable South of England, who settled down as small farmers and tradesmen in western Kentucky, around Paducah, after arriving in the eighteenth century. His father's family, on the other hand, were the mysterious Wisemans. Christian Wiseman arrived in Virginia in 1820, having stowed away with his younger brother on a ship from Hamburg. We know that he was born in Stuttgart, but we know nothing else about him, his early life, or his family, except that they were devout Catholics. The Wiseman brothers settled in west-central Kentucky around Elizabethtown, and the family stayed there until the great migrations that followed WWII. The Wisemans were largely tradesmen and consistently lower middle-class. My grandfather met my grandmother during the war, just before his tour in the navy began, and he left the Church when he married her. To escape his overbearing and disapproving mother, they moved to Oklahoma and later settled in Dallas.

My grandmother attended some college classes, and one of my mother's great-aunts graduated with a teaching degree from Howard Payne University, but those were my parents' only predecessors with any college education. My father studied communications at Baylor, and my mother graduated with a degree in English from Hardin-Simmons, both Baptist universities in central Texas. Both went on to work in media, my father first in radio before settling in as a writer for newspapers, magazines, and now the internet. My mother went directly to newspapers, though she would later return to school for an M.A. in technical writing from Texas Tech University, which led her to teaching in various capacities.

I was born on November 24, 1989, twelve days late and the day after Thanksgiving. Soon thereafter, I was swept into the loving arms of Crestview Baptist Church in Midland, Texas, where my parents proudly presented and dedicated me to God.

We were deeply engaged and devout Baptists. My parents had been leading social groups and Sunday schools since before my older sister, Melody, was born; they were often in choirs and always brought a casserole to Wednesday night fellowship. More importantly, they were real believers and thoughtful in their belief. I do not remember doing family devotionals, but I distinctly remember interrupting my mother's prayer time, praying before meals, and learning about the faith.

My parents were both raised in the Baptist church. My mother, deeply devout, was dedicated to the church from an early age and was committed to her local church in Big Spring, Texas. Her faith and intellect have always been very Texan. She was a commonsense realist without ever having read Thomas Reid and was accused of being a devotee of Francis Schaeffer without ever having read him. She is intellectually rigorous and morally merciful. My father grew up in First Baptist, Dallas, and while the Wisemans were not in church as often as the Davidsons, they were solidly Christian. My father's devotion grew as he learned guitar and began playing occasionally in churches while in college. He would go on to work for Christian radio stations and lead the singles' group at church as a young man. His is the artistic soul of Christianity—a musician who writes songs of praise—and his rendition of "There Is a Fountain Filled with Blood" is deeply engraved on my heart.

Predictably, the Bible was very much at the center of my family's faith. That is, after all, the Baptist tradition: that God is principally revealed to the church in Scripture, which is interpreted by individual Christians under the guidance of the Holy Spirit. I have not attended a Baptist service in nearly twenty years, yet I still find that Scripture comes to my mind most often in the language of the New King James Version, used by most conservative Baptists in the 1990s. Just as we were not aware of our Scottish commonsense realism, we were not aware of having any tradition of interpretation of Scripture. We had both a philosophy and a tradition, but they were largely "in the water".

Midland was a very Baptist place. An oil town and a young city even by American standards, it was set on the southern High Plains. Specifically, we were on the Llano Estacado: the Staked Plane, one of the flattest places on earth. I have heard that the Spanish explorers stated that if their Comanche guides had abandoned them there, they would never have found their way out, due to the all-but-complete lack of features to enable them to orient themselves. The very flatness of the place was realist and Baptist, in a way: things were what they seemed, for the most part, and they seemed simple.

From the day I came home from the hospital, I showed myself to be an introvert. As my mother tells the story, my parents put me in a rocking cradle in their room on my first night at home, and I cried and refused to be comforted. When they moved me to a baby bed that did not rock at the other end of the house, I immediately calmed down and went directly to sleep. This was the beginning of a pattern that continued throughout my babyhood: I wanted to be fed, changed, and then put down—and not bothered with cuddles and play.

I could not tell you what my earliest memory is, but the images of my young childhood are a mosaic of simple sweetness. I think with particular fondness of Mrs. Baird's bread store, where we would walk for sandwich bread and, on occasion, pecan pinwheels or cinnamon buns. I remember being quite small and playing out in the country at the house of fellow parishioners and distant cousins of my mother's, the Orr family, though my distinct memory of their home is cemented by a time when they invited us to a pool party. I sucked my thumb almost constantly at that time, and at this party a wasp lighted on my preferred thumb and stung me. I also remember walking the four blocks to church on Sunday mornings in nice weather. My young childhood was in most ways idyllic, classically American, lower middle-class. But two things became apparent early on: I was precocious, and I had a very short fuse and a violent temper.

My love of the Bible and my aptitude for studying it showed in other early memories. There is an incident that I do not remember but that my parents love to recount: one night at bedtime when I was about seven years old, I told my mother that when I grew up, I wanted to translate the Gospel of Matthew into Hebrew. My seven-year-old naivete, along with boyish desires to be a fireman like my granddaddy or a cowboy like my uncle or a writer like my dad, aside, I already had a desire to study the Bible—and what's more, to translate it with apostolic intent.

I remember, though only vaguely, a more obnoxious, but perhaps more telling, story from about the same time. In Sunday school at the Baptist church, we were learning one of the most traditional lessons: the story of Noah's ark. The teacher told the class that Noah brought two of each kind of animal onto the ark, and seven-year-old Matthew took it upon himself to correct her, pointing out that there were only two of the unclean animals, but seven of the clean. Naturally, I had no notion of the significance of the distinction and did not understand the word "pedantry" or why my teacher was annoyed with me. If I prove to be a self-congratulating know-it-all in the pages that follow, at least the reader can take comfort in the knowledge that I seem to have been such from a very early age.

When I came of school age, my mother began tutoring me at home, in accord with a tradition older than we knew. My older sister had briefly attended our church's preschool, where she thrived. While she, a well-adjusted and social person, often chafed under the comparative isolation of homeschooling, I thrived with the independence, the quiet, and the solitary work. I particularly took to reading, and I remember doing *Sing, Spell, Read, and Write* at the kitchen table, moving a little magnetic car along the chart on our refrigerator as I progressed. It was exhilarating. I have heard language learning described as exciting because it is like learning a secret code. For me, it was like discovering magic. I experienced written language not as a secret but as signs and wonders.

It was at this time that I had the first two of my strange, providential encounters with Catholic grace. God haunted me with Catholicism from my earliest memories. I firmly believe that He haunted me even before I remember, but to that I can bear no account. At the age of six, I asked to be baptized. I do not know what impelled me to ask, and it may have been mere social pressure—that this was what people did—as I have always had an intense desire for belonging, to be a member in the Pauline sense. What I remember clearly is the seriousness with which my parents took my request. They called me into their bedroom in the evening to speak about it, and my mother asked me, "Do you know what Baptism is?" I answered with a profoundly sacramental view of Baptism that I did not understand: "It's being saved."

My parents went on to explain the Baptist view of Baptism: that it is a symbol and public declaration of the salvation that has already occurred through the believer's acceptance, in prayer, of Christ as Lord and Savior. They then led me, completely abashed, in the Sinner's Prayer, and the next week began the process of preparing me for Baptism. I only vaguely remember speaking with the pastor, but I distinctly remember walking down the hallway next to the church library afterward. A copy of *The Rainbow Fish* was on display in the window. The image of the sparkling fish on the cover is engraved on my mind, though I was not conscious of the fish's connection with the Sign of Jonah, with the fish of the sea, and with the baptism of the Children of Israel in the Red Sea. And yet it shimmers in my mind as I recall the day my parents, my pastor, and I planned my Baptism.

The fact that I made it clear when I requested Baptism that I did not understand what it meant in my tradition and that I had to be coached into repeating words I did not very clearly comprehend indicates that my parents and my pastor probably, according to their own rules, should not have baptized me then. It is a strain to call this a "believer Baptism".

In an interview, singer Rich Mullins answered the question "When did you become a Christian?" by describing the events that led to his Baptism in the third grade. When the interviewer, an Evangelical, said that she was asking not about Baptism but about when he was saved, he responded that at Baptism his sins were taken away and he was given the Holy Spirit, which sounds a lot like being saved. The interviewer clarified that she was asking about when he first understood it, and he answered, "Lady, I don't understand it now!"[2] In a similar way, God's prevenient grace intervened despite my lack of understanding, despite my whole church's lack of understanding, and I was baptized as little more than an infant. At the age of six, I died with Christ and was raised with Him.

It was about this time that I wrote my first chorus:

Feel the feel to be free,
Feel the feel to be free,
When you're sitting on Jesus' knee,
Feel the feel to be free.

My next encounter with Catholicism at an early age came with my learning to read chapter books. My mother and I were taking turns reading pages from *The Lion, the Witch, and the Wardrobe* on the couch in our den. The book was a tattered copy that my father had bought when he was a young man himself. I vividly recall the black-and-white illustrations by Pauline Baynes. When we reached the end of a chapter, my mother told me she needed to go prepare dinner. Enthralled by C. S. Lewis' fairy tale, I begged her to keep reading with me, afraid to continue into Faerie alone, but she told me that if I wanted to go further, I needed to do it by myself. When my mother got up, I hesitated and then forged ahead, "further up and further in".

I did not know the Arthurian vocabulary that Lewis was using, and I did not understand the bold, heraldic colors of medieval Catholicism that illuminated every page of the Chronicles of Narnia, but I was enchanted by this

[2] I have not been able to locate this interview again. The only source I can find for it is by the otherwise anonymous "Deborah" of a blog titled *Rich Mullins*: http://richmullinspirituality.blogspot.com/p/baptism.html.

Chanson de Aslan. The "riot of colour" that blazoned the pre-Reformation cathedrals of England, the Dowry of Mary, was flung wildly about me. It is C. S. Lewis who painted the murals on the walls of my mind. It may be controversial to call this a Catholic influence, and it was far from unusual in our Evangelical setting, but there is no denying that the shape of Lewis' fiction is deeply formed by pre-Reformation England. Encounters with prevenient grace are not rare; I am not special for having them. They are the rule, not the exception, and the grace of God is ubiquitous, but we hardly ever allow ourselves to be aware of it.

I have since read *The Lion, the Witch, and the Wardrobe* more times than I can count. A few years after this first encounter with Lewis, I spent a significant amount of my hard-earned allowance to buy a rare copy of *Boxen*, the stories he wrote as a child. As I grew, my love for Lewis grew to include his more grown-up works, both fiction and nonfiction, and some of those will play important roles in this story. Beyond his own influence, my love for "Jack" early on was important because it prepared me for other influences. I first read Tolkien because I knew of nothing else that satisfied the itch left in me by Narnia, and I was eager to read Dorothy Sayers and G. K. Chesterton in part because they were generally associated with Lewis, as either peers or influences. But more on them soon.

2

At some point in these early years, my family traveled to Kentucky to attend a funeral of one of my father's people. I do not recall whose funeral it was, largely because this branch of the family lived much farther from us than my mother's side, so I was not on intimate terms with any of them. My parents tell me it was likely the funeral of my great-uncle Newell. But I distinctly remember that it was a Catholic funeral. I remember the hard wooden pews and the creaking ancient floorboards, quite unlike the modern churches with cushions and concrete floors I was used to. I remember everyone going up for Communion and my grandfather gesturing for us to remain seated. That is the only part of the experience that stayed with me, this distinction between us and the others that I could not comprehend.

I have memories of another Catholic funeral that took place in Midland, but even though I am fairly certain it happened later, my impressions of it are even more vague than that of my relative's funeral. I am not even confident of how I know it was Catholic except that the word is indelibly connected with vague images of a casket in a small, strange chapel.

The next few years were spiritually uneventful, as my family continued attending Crestview Baptist Church. My mother continued homeschooling us, and it is to her tutelage that I attribute most of my academic success. Not only did she teach my sister and me our subjects, and did that well, but she was passionate about teaching us how to think rationally and critically and about sharing her all-but-endless curiosity. The latter welled up in her and, quite naturally and without effort, spilled over onto those around her. She wanted to know, she took nothing for granted, and she took no prisoners. Anything that did not make sense to her was interrogated until it explained itself. She believes in authority but requires that it give good reasons.

When I was perhaps nine years old, our family moved to a new house only a couple of miles away, along the same thoroughfare. This signaled the beginning of many changes to come. It was also the occasion of my next providential encounter with Catholicism. Our new neighbor, the widowed Mrs. Mueller, was a devout Catholic and a member of St. Ann's parish, one of the oldest and most visible parishes in town. Unbeknownst to me, easily half of the city was Catholic, but they were heavily Hispanic, and while we had no disdain for the Spanish-speaking community, we Baptists thought of Catholicism as more a cultural quirk than a serious theological position. Mrs. Mueller was that strange creature that embarrassed us: a northern European Catholic, without even the excuse of being Irish!

She was the most loving soul. I have very few distinct memories of her, but I remember her kindness and her patience quite clearly. In some ways, the handful of times I was in her house—usually when her granddaughters, who were near my age, were over—left more of an impression on me. I had never seen icons or crucifixes, and I certainly did not understand what a devotional candle was, much less a rosary or a holy-water font, but Mrs. Mueller had all of these, and they were intriguing. Who would not be fascinated by these alien objects and their aura of mystery? Encountering them was like walking into one of those labyrinthine antique shops and finding a trove of Hindu ritual objects whose meaning is entirely foreign and whose purpose is obscure. They did not impress themselves upon me as sacred as much as arcane and alluring. I was afraid but was bursting with questions. And there seemed a discontinuity between these awful mysteries and the dear Mrs. Mueller.

Aside from the religious atmosphere of the house, I remember seeing Mrs. Mueller's son sitting at the kitchen table drinking a beer. Cold fear ran down my spine. As a good, teetotaling Baptist, I was under the impression that everyone who drank was an angry drunk in a broken family. But Mr. Mueller sat there looking as agreeable as ever. Stranger still, the beer belonged to his mother, this godly, normal woman who did not at all smell of danger! I did not know how to interpret these events until years later.

Around this time, another event occurred that planted seeds of things to come. Some years before, my father had first heard the music of Rich Mullins on the radio, and being both an ardent musician and a devout Christian who was generally disappointed by the music on Christian radio, he immediately saw that this artist was something different. It was the beginning of a long-term love affair that he passed on to me. Mullins was unusual in contemporary Christian music in more ways than one. Though a Protestant, he was drawn to the tradition of the ancient Church, and he even wrote songs based on the liturgy—notably "Creed" and "Peace: A Communion Blessing from St. Joseph's Square". The first half of his album *A Liturgy, a Legacy, and a Ragamuffin Band*, in fact, is a brief exploration of the major movements of the Mass. Mullins attended a full course of RCIA, and though he never converted, he spent the last years of his life regularly attending daily Mass.[1]

[1] See James Bryan Smith, *Rich Mullins: An Arrow Pointing to Heaven* (Nashville: B&H Publishing Group, 2000).

But in 1997, at age forty-one, he died tragically in a car accident. Just months earlier, my parents had packed my sister and me into the car in our pajamas and driven us two hours to Lubbock to see him perform. I do not remember the news the day he died, but I have stark memories of the episode of *20 The Countdown Magazine* that commemorated his life and work. The meditation on his premature death brought me to tears. My lovely sister tried to comfort me with a card she addressed to me from Rich Mullins as his "biggest fan". Her big heart was in the right place, but I was not comforted. I did not feel like a fan of his at all. I was broken by the tragedy of it—not because I was connected to the man but because he was a man, and he was dead, and I was overwhelmed. Death was so big—too big for an eight-year-old.

My dad bought a copy of that special on CD, and I listened to it over and over through the years. Without looking it up, I can tell you that Rich said in the interviews he did before his death, "This is what liturgy offers that all the razzmatazz of our modern worship can't touch. You don't go home from church going, 'Oh I am just moved to tears.' You go home from church going, 'Wow, I just took communion and you know what? If Augustine were alive today, he would have had it with me and maybe he is and maybe he did.' "[2] I know he told Jon Rivers, former host of *20 The Countdown Magazine*, that Rivers should read Chesterton's *Orthodoxy*, that he loved *The Ragamuffin Gospel* by the laicized priest Brennan Manning, and that he formed an informal group of students of Saint Francis called the Kid Brothers of Saint Frank.

[2] Jimmy Abegg, "Jimmy Abegg—Reflections of Rich", *CCM Magazine*, September 15, 2017, www.ccmmagazine.com/features/jimmy-abegg-reflections-of-rich.

Mullins said, "One day there will be a judgment. One day God will destroy injustice. And because we have a loving and a forgiving Father, maybe we'll survive it. But if we don't, sometimes I think Hell is better than what we deserve, anyway." He made me aware of the darkness inside me and the justice of destruction. He wrote something that I quote to every class of students I teach: "The Bible is not a book for the faint of heart. It is a book full of all the greed and glory and violence and tenderness and sex and betrayal that benefits mankind. It is not the collection of pretty little anecdotes mouthed by pious little church-mice. It does not so much nibble at our shoe-leathers as it cuts to the heart, and splits the marrow from bone to bone. It does not give us answers fitted to our small-minded questions, but truth that goes beyond what we even know to ask."[3]

This was a profoundly large Christianity and a God who had real depth, real weight, real substance. I was not accustomed to people talking about life and death and God in this way, as if these were profoundly eminent concerns. This Christ had flesh and bones. I didn't know who Augustine was, or even G.K. Chesterton, and I hardly knew the name Saint Francis, but when I met them later in my life, I approached them eagerly, as if to say, "I know who you are. You're a friend of Rich's."

My family's first years at the new house were also the most intense years of my fiction writing. I was convinced I wanted to be a writer like my father and like my hero C.S. Lewis, so I produced reams of fiction. Much of it was, of course, fantasy. There was a Hobbit-inspired book about little tailed creatures with hoods whose name I forget, animal stories inspired by the creatures of Redwall

[3] Rich Mullins, "The World as Best as I Remember It", album booklet.

Abbey, and a great dragon epic, *Doraleln*, partly inspired by Stephen R. Lawhead's Dragon King trilogy. But there was also a series of detective stories, inspired by Father Brown and Sherlock Holmes, and a historical epic about the last days of the American Civil War that played out on a fictional island in the North Atlantic, heavily dependent on the historical fiction of Michael and Jeff Shaara.

I had been a Bible reader from early on. I attached great importance and prestige to it, and I was ambitious as well as devout, so I devoured the Good Book. Most of it I could understand, even if it was not as engaging as my fairy tales. I have my first memory of reading Saint Paul at the age of nine or ten and being deeply confounded. I experienced the same thing with Psalms. Genesis and Matthew, Kings and Acts were straightforward narratives, and if there were a few events in them that I did not quite grasp, I understood the progression and most of the events. But these other texts were impossible. Saint Paul had causal clauses whose connection with what preceded and what followed seemed tenuous at best, and I could not comprehend his reasoning. Psalms likewise twisted and turned, with no obvious unity. I knew I was bright and a good reader—though I almost certainly overestimated my abilities—but these I recognized as texts beyond me. I did not have the skill set to understand them, and this, along with Rich Mullins' comments, planted an idea in me that the Bible is not always as straightforward as people make it out to be. I was at least a grade or two ahead in reading, yet I was completely stumped by Saint Paul, and that had to mean something. This book required some explanation. So I gave up on Paul and on Psalms and reserved them for when I was a little older and a little wiser.

At about that same time, my family became dissatisfied with the traditional model of attending church together as a family followed by Sunday school divided by age. My parents were our primary teachers and felt it made the most sense to extend that to religious education. Families should be together, but my parents were unwilling to make us come to an adult class where we would be apart from other children. They wanted a family Sunday school setting. Our days at Crestview Baptist Church were numbered.

First Baptist Church of Midland, Texas, intended to plant a new church on the expanding western end of town, and my parents saw this new beginning as an opportunity to carry out their ideas about family Sunday school. But first we traveled all around West Texas visiting churches, sometimes with the idea of possibly joining them and sometimes just to see how they did things. With the constant change, uncertainty and lack of routine, and new people to navigate every week, this was an intensely draining time for me, an introvert with what would turn out to be a nascent anxiety disorder. My golden childhood was over, and I felt myself in a cold world with an icy, disorienting wind. Crestview had been my sacred geography, and separated from it, I was off the map of the world, but I could not have anticipated the disorientation and reorientation that would follow, the unmaking of my world and remaking it with new sacred directions, new ways, and a new compass.

By comparison with this year of turmoil, the strange newness of regularly attending First Baptist was a welcome relief and a return to a semblance of normalcy. In fact, I already knew many of the faces there through our extensive activity in homeschooling groups. The church was grander and more elaborate than Crestview—in fact, I did not know it, but it was built on a basilica model, the classical form of Roman churches beginning in the fourth century, with Spanish mission influences—and from the outside, it looked quite magisterial, but the patterns were familiar. I did not sense the temporary nature of this arrangement, but we were there for the new church and soon would be uprooted again.

The new plant was begun under the early-2000's name Stonegate Fellowship. It was a Southern Baptist Church, and blessedly, many of our homeschooling friends from First Baptist went over as well. It was a quintessentially "cool" church—the pastor preached from a barstool and the praise band had a drum cage—but sincerely devout and honestly loving. We stayed there more than a year, and my mother recalls it as a time when I "really worshipped". I was intensely aware of my sins and my need for salvation from myself. But the church was not what my parents had hoped it would be. Rather than a family Sunday school, there was a children's church, so most of the young people were not even present during the church service with their parents. In the end, my parents were not able to get approval for a family Sunday school and were demoralized by the whole experience.

In their exploration of family options, my mom and dad had encountered the idea of house churches, and as they grew disillusioned with Stonegate, church at home became gradually more prominent in their minds. Finally, after a particularly frustrating week at Stonegate, when Dad wondered to himself, "Whatever happened to 'I was *glad* when they said unto me, Let us go into the house of the LORD'?",[4] they took the leap, and we stayed at home for church on a Sunday when I was eleven. It was still Baptist, and perhaps even more historically Baptist than the large churches we had been attending. We sang hymns and praise songs to the dulcet tones of Dad's guitar; then we read a passage of Scripture, and Dad said a few words about

[4] Ps 122:1, emphasis added.

it. There was no offertory and no altar call, since it was just the four of us, but that was all that was really different.

I feel I should say something here about 9/11, but I cannot clearly place it along this timeline, which is entirely relative in my mind and tied to exceedingly few dates. The attack of 9/11 seemed to take place in another world from my spiritual development. Even as I watched the coverage on television that fateful morning, it seemed immensely remote from everything that really concerned me, and because it happened during school hours, it is tied in my memory more to school than to church. I believe we were still at Stonegate because I have vague memories of its being mentioned in church that week and of a moving sermon on the subject, all of whose details have escaped me. For me, little changed. I had no uncles or cousins and very few acquaintances of military age. Rising oil prices did, however, send the city of Midland, an oil town, into an economic boom that lasted for the rest of my childhood and youth and indirectly affected my life in ways I did not understand at the time.

As far as I was concerned, this was the summer of Eusebius. I wanted to understand the history of the religion I professed, and my parents had a copy of the fourth-century writer's *Ecclesiastical History* on the shelves. With little context and no guidance, I did not understand it particularly well, but I read it cover to cover in the summer of my eleventh year. And I came away with a great, and entirely undeserved, feeling of superiority. I afterward moved on to Josephus' *History of the Jews*, but I found him too long-winded and dull for even an ambitious young man like me, and I gave up after the first book or two.

Though the turn of the millennium and the beginning of the War on Terror hardly touched me personally, they breathed new life into the flagging apocalypticism of the

Evangelical and Restorationist worlds. Y2K had passed without event, and people had almost given up on the end of the world. But now, it was the end of the world as we knew it, and for many, it seemed that the old answers were no longer enough. I remember staring out our back window and dreading the apocalypse in what may have been an early anxiety attack, wondering what would become of our family dog after the Rapture. My chest tightened, and my vision narrowed to a small patch with large fields of blurry darkness around it. I shook. Something was ending, and as we clung ever closer to our Bibles, a seed of something different, something more ancient, was about to sprout from them.

It was about this time that we made our first remarkable trip overseas—to Papua New Guinea to visit Bible translators. Because we were no longer attending a church, we needed some other ministry to give our tithe to. As ardent readers of missionary stories, my parents decided to adopt a Wycliffe translator and were paired with a family in Koluwawa on Fergusson Island, Papua New Guinea. When, about a year later, they were publishing their first full book, the Gospel of Mark, we offered to come to the dedication. So the four of us boarded an airplane for the twelve-hour flight from Los Angeles to Sydney, Australia, and then over to Port Moresby, where we took a commuter plane out to the tiny island where the translators lived. It was the first time I had been on a plane so small that the attendants had to direct passengers where to sit in order to maintain a proper balance. It was also the first and last time I have been on a plane with a crate of live chickens.

We boarded the plane on the tarmac, and as we took off from the simple but familiar airport in Port Moresby, we left behind everything reminiscent of home. The island was north, across the Papuan Peninsula, with its great green mountains covered in rainforest. About the time we reached cruising altitude, we would begin our next descent because this was a commuter and functioned more like a bus than a flight. In an extremely mountainous developing country, road building takes a long time to catch up to the demand for travel, but Papua New Guinea had a transportation windfall in the form of hundreds of WWII airstrips dotting the country. Instead of making the arduous trek through the forest and over the mountains, commuters use small prop planes that hop from one airstrip to the next, touching down every twenty minutes or so in loops out from the city and back. Because they function as bus stops, these airfields look like bus stops: a simple shelter next to a grass strip, surrounded by rainforest, where the pilot is the only official, handling the baggage as well as taking payment, either in cash or in goods.

We finally set down on an island neighboring our destination, where we were met by the missionaries. They met us with unripe coconut milk, a local delicacy, and we clambered into boats with outboard motors to cross the wide bay to the next island. There we caught our first sight of flying fish as they swept up from the sea, flew for what seemed dozens of yards, and then gracefully dove back down. The boatmen joked that our life jackets were pointless because if we fell in there, the sharks would get us before anyone could rescue us. Even the missionaries were not entirely sure how serious they were.

There followed a week of meeting people, walking through the rainforest, snorkeling over pristine corals, and, finally, attending a great party outdoors to celebrate the published version of the Gospel of Mark. The people had been converted decades before by earlier missionaries, and there were already three churches of different denominations in the area. We could hear the charismatic church's services from miles away as they sang late into the night, hymns resonating over and through the jungle. Like anywhere else, the churches had controversies between them over theological issues, and the debate could apparently get heated, but on this day, all that was put aside as they sang a song, written for the occasion, about the "United Ekklesia of Koluwawa", which came together to celebrate their new Gospel.

The dedication was incredibly moving, and we were treated as guests of honor. But I was more interested in the conversations that happened back in the missionaries' house in the evenings. Some other missionaries had been evacuated from their station because of threats from bandits—whom the locals referred to as "rascals"—and were staying with these translators. They discussed translation problems about literal and dynamic translation, whether they should interpret and explain the text in the body of the text itself or save that information for footnotes and parentheticals. For long afternoons on the mosquito-netted porch set on high wooden beams above the jungle, they discussed the fact that their two projects were more closely related than they had thought, amounting to mere dialects of the same language, not long separated. It was my first taste of linguistics and of the Bible translation I had dreamed of as a child, and I was riveted.

Part II

Sinai (2002–2008)

3

Appropriately, our entrance into the Hebrew Roots Movement was brought about by a return to a different kind of roots. While we were having church at home, my family felt the need to make sure we did not "forsake the assembling", as Hebrews 10:25 warns, so we made efforts to gather regularly with other believers, especially those on the fringes like us. When news reached us that some old acquaintances from Crestview, the B—— family, were also moving toward church at home, we were quick to make a connection.

I do not know whether my parents or Mr. and Mrs. B—— reached out first, but both families were eager for fellowship. The B—— family were slightly younger. Their oldest, a boy, was just a few months younger than I was, and he was followed by two daughters. They would eventually be joined by two more sons. Our Sunday mornings remained mostly a family affair, but we had frequent dinners, often accompanied by singing along to Dad's guitar, either at the B—— house or at ours, and Taco Tuesdays at Rosa's Café.

Mr. B—— was already interested in the Hebrew Roots Movement, which may require some explanation. It is difficult to summarize the movement briefly because it is diverse, which will become significant as this history proceeds. The one commonality of the entire movement is an attempt to frame New Testament Christianity in the Jewish setting of Jesus and the apostles, and its members have concluded that this involves observing the Law of Moses, the Torah, in some way. Beyond that, there are few universals. Whether Torah observance means following traditional Jewish interpretations of Moses or attempting to find your own based on Scripture alone; whether the members are trinitarian or even believe that Christ is divine; which books are canonical; what language the New Testament was written in—all these are controversial.

Mr. B—— himself was in many ways an orthodox Protestant: he believed in the authority of Scripture alone—in fact, he read only the King James Version throughout my youth—and was concerned that the Baptists had not gone far enough in rooting out pagan accretions from the Catholic Middle Ages. He was fiercely libertarian, and for my birthday one year, he gave me a copy of *The Law* by Frédéric Bastiat, a book I devoured. This radical independence and individualism were at the heart of Mr. B——'s Hebrew Roots study: he did not want to rely on the mere conventions of the Baptist church but wanted to delve into Scripture for himself, working to place it in its proper historical context without dependence on any tradition. He was a man of West Texas, much like my mother's staunchly libertarian family.

This libertarian individualism was a continuous undertone of much of the Hebrew Roots Movement in West Texas. To an extent, it was an appeal to the Law of Moses because nobody but God Himself could tell a free citizen what to do. "No king but King Jesus", as the old slogan goes.

I was not privy to the early conversations Mr. B—— and my parents had about the Jewish roots of Christianity, though I vaguely remember dinner-table conversations about a seventh-day Sabbath. My first real awareness of what was going on came when Mr. B—— lent us a DVD about biblical feasts, in which a man with a full beard and long gray hair and wearing a long tunic and something that looked like a purple poncho over it, with a round cap on his head, explained the feasts and fasts of Leviticus 23. The man was Michael Rood, and the essential premise of the video was that Jesus, whom he called by His Aramaic name, Yeshua, had fulfilled the spring cycle of feasts—Passover or Unleavened Bread, Firstfruits, and Shavuot or Pentecost—in His Incarnation, death, and Resurrection, and therefore He would fulfill the fall cycle—the feast of Trumpets or Rosh Hashanah, the Day of Atonement, and the feast of Tabernacles—on His return. The implication of this understanding was that Christians should therefore observe these feasts, the former as a remembrance of Christ's coming and the latter as an anticipation of His return. If some of the feasts remained unfulfilled, how could we excuse not observing them, since the Israelites were commanded to observe them all in anticipation of the Messiah?

Those of my readers who know the theology of the Epistle to the Hebrews will have objections here, but I would not discover those objections for several more years, so we will pass over them without mention here. We found this argument quite compelling at the time. In fact, it fed into our desire for roots, for primitiveness of religion, and our nascent apocalypticism. It handed us something ancient with the prediction of something eminent. Michael Rood was firmly convinced that the fulfillment of the fall feasts was coming soon and that part of being ready for that great day meant returning to the observance of these holy days, just as observing the spring feasts had been part of Israel's preparation for the Incarnation.

Rood's argument was interesting, but what it implied for us took some time to work out. It was not immediately obvious from that video, for instance, that the argument was relevant to anything other than the holy days. At the same time, Rood did not make a purely positive case for celebrating the Mosaic calendar; he also made a negative case against traditional Christian celebrations, claiming they were of pagan origin and therefore biblically illicit. It was the front edge of a distinction that would loom large over the years that followed, between "Hebrew thinking" and "Greek thinking".

Once we had accepted this basic premise, things began to move very quickly over the next year, from early 2002 through early 2003. I turned thirteen during this first, rapidly changing year. I remember distinctly the moment when I decided that if I was going to observe these holy days, if Michael Rood was right about that, then I also needed to keep kosher—that is to say, to follow the Bible's food laws. We took our china plates out to the dumpster and shattered them because, according to Leviticus 11:33, earthenware that comes into contact with unclean food must be shattered. I have a photo of me and several of the B—— children on Rosh Hashanah, wearing white, sighting the new moon, and ready to eat the traditional apples with honey. At Passover we ate lamb, and though we did not do the slaughtering, we managed to extract some blood from the leg of lamb and used a paintbrush to put it on the door of the B—— house.

Michael Rood loomed large over these early days of our entry to the Hebrew Roots Movement. But in order for you to understand the significance of that influence, I need to explain briefly a sectarian dispute that emerged in medieval Judaism. Since the Second Temple period, between 516 B.C. and A.D. 70, there have been disputes about how to interpret the Torah, the books of Moses. Many Christians are at least vaguely familiar with the major schools of thought during Christ's ministry: the Pharisees, who were predominant and laid the foundation for the later rabbinical schools that gave us traditional Judaism; the Sadducees, who controlled the priesthood but not public belief and practice and rejected all of the canon except the books of Moses; the mystical, desert-dwelling Essenes; and the syncretizing Hellenists, who read the Bible allegorically and gave us Philo of Alexandria.[1]

After the destruction of the Temple in A.D. 70, this sectarianism decreased, and a broad orthodoxy emerged under the rabbinical schools in Babylon and Galilee. These schools interpreted the Law of Moses with the aid of an oral tradition that was a combination of laws and customs passed down from antiquity and jurisprudential decisions of the Jewish courts concerning the application of both the written law and the oral customs. This lore, known as the Oral Torah, was gradually compiled first in a book called the Mishnah and then in a series of debates and commentaries on the Mishnah, called the Gemara. The two combined make up the Talmud.[2] But a new controversy emerged at the end of the eighth century and the beginning of the ninth. The controversy was begun by a Jewish man living in Babylon named Anan Ben David.

Anan Ben David disagreed with the broad consensus that had emerged regarding Jewish tradition and took it upon himself to write his own exhaustive work on Jewish law, belief, and practice: the Sefer HaMitzvot, or Book of Commandments. Exactly what Ben David was trying to accomplish with this work is sometimes disputed, but

[1] For a mildly outdated but thorough overview of the situation at about the time of Christ, see E. P. Sanders, *Paul and Palestinian Judaism: A Comparison of Patterns of Religion* (Minneapolis: Fortress Press, 1977).

[2] See Abraham Cohen, *Everyman's Talmud* (New York: E. P. Dutton, 1949), xv–xxxvii.

what happened as a result is a matter of record. He proposed an alternative system of interpretation that relied on logical and literary techniques rather than on the oral tradition, and he recorded his conclusions. His conclusions were largely ignored, but his opposition to the Oral Torah and his reliance on the Hebrew Bible alone as authoritative exploded into the ninth- and tenth-century sect called the Karaites. It was a kind of precursor to the Protestant Reformation, and to former Protestants like us and Michael Rood, it was an enormously appealing alternative to the traditions of Judaism. We were criticizing a Christian tradition that we believed was a later, spurious addition to the gospel and were naturally drawn to a Jewish movement that had performed the same kind of housecleaning. Ben David was followed by a series of scholars, from Jacob al-Kirkisani to Elijah Bashyatchi. They argued for various principles and conclusions on subjects in Jewish Law, but they agreed that the Oral Torah was spurious and that the text of the Hebrew Bible alone was the divinely authorized revelation to Israel.[3]

The Karaites claim descent from the Second Temple Sadducees, just as traditional Judaism claims descent from the Pharisees. The connection is in some ways tenuous, since Josephus says the Sadducees did not accept the books of the Prophets,[4] and the New Testament tells us they did not believe in the resurrection of the dead (see Mt 22:23; Acts 23:6–8), whereas the medieval Karaites accepted both. The Karaites argued that no outside information or tradition was necessary, that readers were capable of interpreting

[3] See Leon Nemoy, *Karaite Anthology: Excerpts from the Early Literature*, Yale Judaica Series, ed. Leon Nemoy, vol. 7 (New Haven: Yale University Press, 1980), xiii–xxvi, 1–11.

[4] Flavius Josephus, *The Works of Flavius Josephus*, trans. William Whiston (London: Nelson, 1875), 13, 10, 6; 18, 1, 2–4.

the Torah for themselves, and that anything that was not clearly specified in the Hebrew Bible was open to different views and different applications. Mr. Rood teamed up early on with a modern Karaite named Nehemia Gordon, a popular writer and speaker who boasted an M.A. in Biblical Studies from the Hebrew University of Jerusalem—an impressive credential. They argued that Jesus was Himself a Karaite who taught His disciples to observe the Torah but rejected the "traditions of the elders", according to Mark 7:8. This partnership would later become very important in my development, but for the moment, we will leave it at the fact that my family accepted this approach to Torah observance from the outset.

Our observance quickly progressed from holy days and dietary laws, or *kashrut*, to include the ritual ornament of fringes, called *tzitziot*—sometimes called "tassels" in English—but using the braided style preferred by the Karaites rather than the wrapped style you may have seen if you are familiar with Jewish religion and culture. In typical Hebrew Roots fashion, we did not attach them to the traditional four-cornered garment, following a literal interpretation of Deuteronomy 22:12; instead, in an analogical interpretation that would have made Anan Ben David proud, we attached them to our belt loops. I began to pray the Shema, a central prayer of Judaism consisting of Deuteronomy 6:4–9 and 11:13–21 and Numbers 15:37–41, twice daily, in the morning and in the evening.

These were halcyon days. We were reading the Bible with new eyes and discovering a wealth of ritual completely foreign to the Southern Baptist tradition. We waited outside to see the new moon marking the beginning of a month or a holy day; we ate ritual meals with our friends late into the night. We prayed every day and built a tight-knit sense of community, and even getting dressed in the morning took on theological significance. A remarkable sense of restoration and almost of magic pervaded everything we did.

Matthew 5:17–20 was a central text for us throughout these years, and it will come up repeatedly, so we need to have it clearly in mind. In the King James, it reads thus:

> Think not that I am come to destroy the law, or the prophets: I am not come to destroy, but to fulfil. For verily I say unto you, Till heaven and earth pass, one jot or one tittle shall in no wise pass from the law, till all be fulfilled. Whosoever therefore shall break one of these least commandments, and shall teach men so, he shall be called the least in the kingdom of heaven: but whosoever shall do and teach them, the same shall be called great in the kingdom of heaven. For I say unto you, That except your righteousness shall exceed the righteousness of the scribes and Pharisees, ye shall in no case enter into the kingdom of heaven.

No text was quoted so frequently as this one in the communities of my youth. We understood this to mean that the entirety of the Torah of Moses applied to our lives in a more or less literal way. But problems presented themselves almost immediately. This passage made it clear that it applied to *all* the commandments, without exception. There was a clear problem, though: Hebrews 7:12 specifically states that there has been a "change ... of the law" with regard to priesthood and sacrifice. We were firmly convinced that the entire Torah applied to our lives, but there was some confusion over this point. In these early days, the solution was not widely disputed because it seemed clear to us that this change applied only to sacrifice and the priesthood, which were henceforth all concentrated in the Messiah and His sacrifice. Everything else applied, at least in theory, to our lives, though there were obvious exceptions regarding commandments that applied specifically to the land of Israel.

While we seemed to have reasonable explanations for all our exceptions, I did feel some discomfort. The Protestant churches of our past also made distinctions of this kind, between the "moral" laws that still applied to our lives and the "ritual" laws that did not. On balance, I thought ours was the better interpretation of these texts because it took more seriously the words of Christ in Matthew 5, which appeared to be neglected by the church. We will return to this text a little later when I first encountered a serious attempt to explain these words of Christ by the Evangelical tradition.

4

As we entered this world of Hebrew Roots, we were introduced to its other members a few at a time. Two or three Bible studies, or “Torah Studies”, as we preferred to call them, stand out. For the first, we met at the house of Mr. R——, a man of Jewish heritage who was partially blind from glaucoma and styled himself a prophet. He taught things that, at the time, I thought were strange. Later I realized they were only repackaged versions of self-help and the prosperity gospel. I distinctly remember the time he claimed that he had sat all day with an angel in his office.

We would meet in his dining room on Friday evenings, or *erev Shabbat*, the eve of the Sabbath, following Jewish practice. There we would sit, my family, his family, and one or two others, around the table deep into the night. It was a kind of mystic time, as we studied, in dim light with candles, the surely coming apocalypse and how the Hebrew Roots community was supposed to weather it. There were Hanukkah menorahs—called hanukkiahs—and a great ram’s horn called a *shofar*. I felt I was being admitted to mysteries. After the Bible study, we would stay even later, and Mr. R—— would serve us the gourmet food he loved to make.

Through his teaching, it became clear to us that observing the Torah necessarily meant living in a community with the same goal. There was a reason the observant Jews tended to gather in large communities: it made it far easier to find kosher food and observe the required rest on the

Sabbath. This idea fed into the intense growing feeling I had that I later named "home-longing". The Welsh call it *hiraeth*. The idea of living in a religious community moved me to the point of pain, like being in love. But it became clear that Mr. R—— had a need for control that was out of proportion. Community with him was out of the question. We attended his meetings off and on for about three years.

Soon we were introduced to another Torah study. This was a very different community in almost every way. At the time, they met in the Sunday school area of a large charismatic church, where the children could run around and play while the adults talked, and off to one side there was always a large table full of snacks that everyone provided. While there were distinctly leading personalities, there was no formal leadership, and the atmosphere was far less traditional but not less apocalyptic. It was more libertarian, with an emphasis on the responsibility of the head of each house to make decisions for the house's observance of the Torah. It was a patriarchal model that was familiar from conservative Baptist environments, but it was presented with a greater emphasis on the Old Testament and its models of family governance.

More importantly from my perspective, there were children, a great many of them. Only one was my age, but a whole passel were younger, and it was a sign of a more living community than the other. I believe it was at this point that my sister began feeling the social strain more than the rest of us. Most of those involved in the movement were young families, and no one local to us was close to her in age. In fact, at two and a half years her junior, I was the closest she had to a peer in the Hebrew Roots Movement. We were still involved in homeschool activities, though, and that gave us a broader base for friendship and socialization. The same year we began exploring

Hebrew Roots, I competed for our homeschool organization's track team in a meet against the area's private schools and took home first place in the eight hundred meter and second place in the four hundred. But our changing rule of life made things difficult. We reserved Saturdays for rest and Bible study; we did not eat unkosher food or anything that had come into contact with it, though we were fairly lax in this observance. Furthermore, the homeschool community was deeply religious, and our divergence from orthodoxy made things uncomfortable.

In this Torah study, I first encountered another book and set of ideas that were a major theme of the Hebrew Roots Movement. The book was *Too Long in the Sun* by Richard Rives, and it claimed that Christianity was overrun with secretly pagan practices that perverted its worship and made it unacceptable to God according to Deuteronomy 18:9. Rives tied most of these supposedly pagan practices to what he claimed were Roman practices related to the worship of Sol Invictus, the sun god. Rives connected Christmas with Saturnalia (despite the name); he followed the ninth-century Christian historian Bede in associating Easter with the supposed goddess Eostre (whom he conveniently connected to the Babylonian Ishtar through the vague resemblance of the names); and he even tied worship on Sunday not to the Resurrection but to the Roman *dies solis*, the Day of the Sun. Christianity was not merely wrong or mistaken; it was fundamentally corrupted and converted into Roman sun worship. It was pagan and corrupt from some early date, usually associated with Constantine the Great.

Though some of these accusations were new, most of them were old and recycled from previous centuries. I swallowed them hook, line, and sinker. My mother the logician, on the other hand, saw a flaw in the arguments from the outset. She noted that, with regard to Easter in particular, Rives' only evidence for the celebration's pagan origin was the "opposition witness" fallacy, based on Bede—a late-comer in the relevant history. The argument was supposed to be stronger because Saint Bede was a Catholic, and so it was against what we assumed were his interests to admit the pagan origin of the name and, by extension, the holiday. Though I dismissed her at the time, my mother pointed out how weak an argument this really was, particularly as it lacked corroboration in other ancient sources. As far as I am aware, none of us did further research, but Mom reached the more sensible conclusion that, while there may have been a kind of "pagan creep" from the surrounding cultures into Christianity, there was no grand conspiracy. Christians were not thinly disguised pagan sun worshippers, though they might be misguided syncretists. I cannot say when, but her arguments eventually had an effect on me and I softened, though I maintained there was more deliberation by parties such as Constantine than she claimed.

Around this time, I stopped reading the Chronicles of Narnia because of Lewis' affection for pagan mythological creatures and gods. At first, I completely repudiated him. Later, after I went off to university, I softened my position, but I was never comfortable with his work again while I remained in the movement. It was extremely painful for me and felt like a divorce, but I could not see how I could rail against Christian paganism and continue reading the Chronicles, rife with river gods and sacred trees.

This group did not continue to meet in the church but soon moved into the homes of its members. One family in particular, the T—— family, had a house in the country. The young people had plenty of room for outdoor play, and the house had a substantial living room where everyone could meet. This group met on Saturday afternoons and ran late into the evening. We began with music, for which Dad was often invited to bring his guitar and play, followed by an exhaustive close reading of the *parashah*, the Hebrew word for "portion". The parashah is the reading from the Torah—traditionally translated "law" but more literally "teaching"—assigned for each week of the year. Traditionally, synagogues make a complete cycle of the Pentateuch every year, in addition to a smaller portion of the Prophets. In recent history, some synagogues have reverted to an older tradition of completing the cycle in three years so that each portion can be given more complete attention. It is one of those elements of the Oral Torah that we consciously adopted as a matter of convenience, though we in principle rejected the authority that established it.

A third group we encountered at this time was led by some old family friends of my mother's in her hometown, about forty-five minutes from our house. This group was similar to the second, except there were fewer children because the young families were very young indeed. It was farther out in the country, and in many ways more familiar, but it had less of an impact on our lives because of the drive.

Over the course of my thirteenth year, we were slowly introduced to the wider Hebrew Roots world through Mr. R——. It was an informal, very low-profile network that was almost impossible to connect with unless you knew someone in the community. Once again, there were frequent long drives around the area for festivals and Sabbaths. Soon we were connected with little Torah Studies throughout West Texas and even began organizing larger meetings for major holy days.

It was about this time that two developments regarding my relationship with literature took place. From some branch of the family—I do not remember which—we inherited a small collection of antique books printed in the 1890s and 1900s. As a bibliophile, I was drawn to these volumes and made it my business to delve into them. One was a collection of Edgar Allan Poe's mystery stories, and another was a collection of southern poets, which also included some Poe. For the first time, I breathed the rapturous air of Romantic poetry. The books intoxicated me, and I quickly committed to memory "Annabel Lee" and "The Bells" by Poe and "The Conquered Banner" by the Confederate chaplain Father Abram Joseph Ryan.

The dark romance of tragedy in these poems spoke to me deeply, and I began to seek out more. I found a collection of favorite American poems and soon memorized many of them—the more tragic, the better. "Casey at the Bat" by Ernest Thayer and "Casabianca" by Felicia Dorothea Hemans were favorites, and I quickly learned them by heart and recited them to myself often. I did not know the Romantics as a school, but I knew them by spirit. I also committed the deeply eloquent Gettysburg Address to memory and did not feel any tension with my love of Father Ryan's poetry.

Somehow, it did not occur to me at the time that I was capable of writing poetry or that I could go looking for any of these authors at the library. I loved our library—it was perfect for bookworms, having been expanded several times through annexation, with the result that there were tight, obscure back rooms and mostly unused balconies in arcane research sections. To me, it will always be the type of what a library ought to be: musty, confusing, labyrinthine, private, quiet, ill planned, and well stocked. There I encountered more of what I loved, but mostly in prose: I devoured Brian Jacques' Redwall books and discovered the strange, gothic Jacobite stories of Joan Aiken's Wolves Chronicles.

The second discovery, which may not have come until my fourteenth year (I cannot be certain), was of the writing of nonfiction. In my writing course in school, I adamantly resisted the idea of having to write a persuasive essay: I was a fiction writer, and at thirteen or fourteen, I had concluded I would write nothing else. But it was required, and I eventually yielded. Putting down on paper in clear form the research, understanding, and argument that I had in a somewhat more disorganized fashion in my mind was no less revelatory and rapturous than the discovery of Poe and Hemans. My focus in writing immediately shifted. I wrote two lengthy and extremely pretentious essays, the first called "On the Worship of Angels", which concerned the disproportionate honor granted to things that are, in themselves, good. The other came out of a long session of brooding on a topic that fascinated me: How did people make others do things against their will, and was that really possible at all? I wrote a long essay titled "On Coercion".

The next stage in our journey involved the feast of Tabernacles. Tabernacles, *Sukkot* in Hebrew, is a fall feast during which the Jewish people commemorate Israel's forty years in the wilderness by living in "booths" or "tabernacles" for seven days. According to Leviticus 23:39–43, the Israelites are commanded to take the branches of trees native to the Holy Land and to "rejoice before the LORD your God for seven days" to commemorate the fact that they lived in tents for forty years. Later, after the Babylonian Exile, Ezra and Nehemiah specify that the tabernacles are to be built out of the branches of most of the same trees (Neh 8:15). Tabernacles is a celebration that completes and contrasts the solemn days that precede it, ending in *Shemini Atzeret*, the eighth great day symbolizing new beginnings. Because its date is not based on the Gregorian or Julian calendars used traditionally in the West, it does not always fall on the same days on those calendars, but it is always in September or October.

In Jewish tradition, this festival is observed quite straightforwardly, by building wooden booths roofed with tree branches, usually palm, and spending time in them every day during Sukkot. People eat and study the Torah in them, and some sleep in them as well. The Hebrew Roots community applied a looser interpretation of these rules, in part relying on the fact that Leviticus 23 does not specifically state that the booths must be made out of tree branches. We tended to go camping. For our first feast of Tabernacles, we simply set up a tent in our backyard. We had friends over for dinner and ate on the back porch, sang songs, and studied the Bible. It was common in this community to celebrate the birth of the Messiah during the feast of Tabernacles, relying on John 1:14, which says in Greek that the Word came and εσκηνωσεν, *eskeinosen*, literally "tented" or "tabernacled" among us. Some took this literally to mean that Yeshua was born during the feast of Tabernacles, while others took it more figuratively.

The second year that we celebrated Sukkot, Mr. R—— had been warning us for a long time of the coming apocalypse and the necessity of being prepared. We were very interested in moving to Israel, in part because we believed that many of the commandments could only be observed there and in part because we believed that a part of "end-time prophecy" was a return of the believers in Yeshua to the Torah and the Holy Land. It was important that God was making a way for us to return to His chosen way of life. Mr. R—— mentioned a movement and an organization for a "Second Exodus", appealing to the language of Jeremiah 16, which promises a new and greater Exodus than that from Egypt.

The organizer of the event was a person with connections in Israeli politics who donated large sums of money to the campaigns of politicians in exchange for hints about a path for Torah-observant believers to become Israeli citizens. It was a clever ruse for the politicians' fundraising, and because nothing definitive was ever promised, it was not too difficult for them to continue manipulating donors. People like the organizer of this event were frequently taken in. Politicians are the same everywhere.

There was supposed to be a major revelation in this regard at this organizer's Sukkot celebration at a state park in Central Texas. Apparently, my parents offended Mr. R—— by going directly to the organizer rather than treating Mr. R—— as our "leader". Our relationship with him cooled after that, though contact continued for several more years. It was our first real experience of the wider Hebrew Roots Movement. I remember pulling into the drive at the riverside park and seeing the event tent, a modest to middling tent but extravagant by our standards, and I was slightly in awe. The tents, campers, trailers, and pop-ups of the movement's members filled the entire spacious campground, and the gathering included groups from West Texas, from the Dallas–Fort Worth area, and—what would become most significant for me down the line—from Houston.

The meetings were familiar, with singing sometimes accompanied by Israeli folk dance (which we knew by the name "Davidic Dance"), though in this venue there were more lectures or "teachings" than discussions, due in part to the size of the gathering. Do not get me wrong: it was not a particularly large gathering, even by Hebrew Roots standards; there were fewer than two hundred people. But it was enormous to me.

I first made the acquaintance of Mssrs. O—— and D—— at this event. Mr. D——— began the week leading the worship music on guitar. He cut an odd figure, even in the Hebrew Roots Movement. He was quite tall, had long hair and an enormous beard, and often wore strange clothing. And he did not merely play the popular minor-key songs with Hebrew words sprinkled in but wrote his own music. I soon learned that he had taken a Nazirite vow. According to Numbers 6, three restrictions apply to the Nazirite: he may not cut his hair or beard; he may not partake of wine or strong drink; and he may not touch any dead, unclean thing. According to Mr. D——, this involved even more restrictions. He did not consume caffeine or soda of any kind, he limited his sugar, and he did not wear any clothing with a visible label or logo. He was a kind of ascetic and decidedly a mystic.

Mr. O—— was the leader of the group from Houston. He wore a skullcap, called a *yarmulke* in Yiddish and a *kippah* in Hebrew. This was unusual in itself, but his was squarer and had more structure than the flat yarmulke with which most are familiar; it was like a pillbox hat. To Westerners, it would be more commonly reminiscent of Islam than of Judaism, though it is common in Jewish communities from the Near East. I later learned it was a kind of kippah that originated with the Jewish communities in Central Asia, but Mr. O—— wore it because it was reminiscent of the miters of the Israelite priesthood. Mr. O—— is a wise man to whom I am indebted for many things. The thing for which I am most grateful is that he never gave me a platform; most others I met did, and it was not helpful to my young mind and ego.

The Houston group was immediately distinct. They were serious about sanctity, about priesthood, about antiquity in clothing and practice, about the laws of modesty called *tzuniut*, and, most unusually, about the laws of ritual purity concerning sex and menstruation. They were interesting for their use of and respect for Jewish traditions, without ever treating them as absolutely authoritative. The traditions were considered venerable but not directly from God, in the way the written Torah was.

The lead speaker arrived midweek and despite my anticipation gave a forgettable speech about how we were all going to return to the Holy Land soon before the coming of the Lord. Nothing ever came of these efforts, though Mr. O—— later came into possession of an apartment in Judea. Something else happened, however, that put us in greater connection with Mr. D——. During one of the teaching sessions, I found that I did not at all agree with the speaker and, in fact, found him quite misleading. I do not remember the topic. The only point I remember was in his introductory remarks; he said that if we were really going to be Hebrew rather than Greek, we should move the chairs into a circle, as for a roundtable, rather than having them in rows, as for a lecture. I could see very little evidence for that idea in either the Old or the New Testament, and it left a bad taste in my mouth. In the end, I left halfway through, trying to sneak out without making a scene. Mr. D—— was elated. He later revealed that God had told him that He had to "send a boy to do a man's job" because Mr. D—— was the one meant to walk out. I was slightly abashed and confused because I had really meant to sneak out without being noticed, but I was also proud, as only a young teenager being praised by adults can be.

I returned home with a renewed excitement about the land of Israel, about the idea of making *aliyah*—that is, becoming an Israeli citizen; literally "to go up" in Hebrew—and about the holiness laws of the Torah. These were always complicated to apply, in part because the rules for our situation, away from the Temple, were unclear, especially as we still did not rely on the Oral Torah for insights. But we made our best effort. It became apparent early on that this was a watershed in the community, between those who made a serious effort to observe the laws of ritual purity and those who did not, and it led in new directions. It was a strain to many, especially the women, and involved a great deal of trial and error.

By this time, I was beginning high school, and it was time to choose my required language course. Because we were homeschooled, the pool was vast, consisting of any language for which a self-teaching curriculum was available. Naturally, I chose to study Hebrew. This did not go well at first because we attempted to use a cutting-edge biblical Hebrew curriculum that involved tapes and conversation. We might have known that, as a deeply introverted bookworm, this would not be my preferred method of learning. It was not until my second year of high school, when we bought a basic modern Hebrew grammar textbook that I could simply read through, that I really began to take off.

Our education was unusual in many ways. Of course, we did the basic things needed. We took algebra I and II and geometry at minimum, though my sister continued into more advanced math. We did a basic course of sciences, though I have strong memories only of biology (which I enjoyed) and chemistry (which I did not). We studied world history from antiquity to modernity, with a distinctly Semitic focus. We had both English composition and English literature, but in a somewhat cursory way. We were intensely focused on Hebrew, Judaism, and the Bible. Ironically, years later, I would read David Carr's *Writing on the Tablet of the Heart* and discover that the Hebrew Bible emerged out of a Jewish effort to create a literary canon to answer the Greek use of Homer. So it is appropriate that I emerged from high school with an intimate knowledge of the Torah, never having read *The Iliad* or *The Odyssey*. But I was deeply moved by *A Tale of Two Cities*: "It is a far, far better thing that I do, than I have ever done; it is a far, far better rest that I go to than I have ever known."[1]

In junior high, I had turned away from track and to swimming. This was primarily out of competitiveness with my older sister, but track had also lost much of its appeal when I could no longer compete in Saturday meets. When I was fourteen, I got my first part-time job teaching swimming lessons to small children. It would be the only job I had in high school or college that I thoroughly enjoyed. I learned that I liked teaching and found it extremely rewarding, and my boss and the children's parents seemed to think I did it well.

Once I knew the Hebrew alphabet and a very little basic grammar, my parents purchased for me a copy of Green's *Interlinear Bible*, which had Hebrew and Greek matched word by word with English translations. Reading whole stories, especially stories I already knew intimately, helped me acquire an understanding of biblical language. But I was about to be met by seriously misleading sources in this regard.

Brad Scott was a popular speaker and teacher in Hebrew Roots circles who taught that Hebrew was essentially a pictographic language. It was an intriguing proposition, which he had learned from a predecessor named Frank T. Seekins and his strangely popular book *Hebrew Word Pictures*. The idea was that each letter of the Hebrew alphabet had both a phonetic and a pictographic value and that Hebrew words could be better understood by reading

[1] Charles Dickens, *A Tale of Two Cities* (London: James Nisbet and Co., 1902), 454.

the pictographs that gave their true, core meaning. Mr. Scott stressed that these symbols were the key to adopting "Hebrew thinking" as opposed to "Greek thinking".

It is not disputed that the Hebrew alphabet is distantly descended from Egyptian pictographic hieroglyphs. The shapes of the letters in the alphabet's earliest form, the Proto-Sinaitic script, are clearly crude adaptations of Egyptian writing into an alphabet.[2] What Seekins and Scott claimed was that those pictographic symbols were still meaningful for the understanding of alphabetic Hebrew. This made the interpretation of every sentence a kind of code breaking. It was an exciting new way to find secret meanings in the Bible, but it was not the magic I had fallen in love with as a child. I was not excited by codes; I was excited by spirit and fire. So, while I pursued this understanding of Hebrew for about two years, I was by disposition inclined to drop it as soon as the reasonable arguments against it were presented, and it did not feature largely in my study of the Bible.

A local Christian television station, God's Learning Channel, had invited Brad to speak, and my family and I, along with other members of the Hebrew Roots community, met him afterward at the studio. This station loomed large in our consciousness. The producers frequently invited Hebrew Roots speakers and aired instructional programs by Jewish teachers. The station was a source to which we constantly referred but was also a source of controversy. Some of the teachers denied the divinity of Christ, some denied His Messiahship, some firmly defended traditional Judaism, and some vociferously repudiated it, though the

[2] See W. F. Albright, "The Early Alphabetic Inscriptions from Sinai and Their Decipherment", *Bulletin of the American Schools of Oriental Research*, no. 110 (April 1948): 6–22.

latter gradually lost favor as the traditional party took hold. Years later, one of our local leaders gained favor and was invited to be on their shows, though this was after I had moved away, so I do not know any of the details.

This television station introduced us to a world of Judaism and of Hebrew Roots thought that we would not otherwise have had access to, and their bookstore was a treasure trove of information, as well as Israeli imports and Judaica. That shop left a deep impression on my mind, like some ancient bazaar or trading post with stacks of books in parallel Hebrew and English, along narrow aisles, among pungent smells of anointing oils and olive wood. They sold fabrics and curios and foods, all of Middle Eastern origin to some degree or another, a feast for the senses of a curious boy.

5

About this time, Mom set her sights on creating a humanities curriculum for Hebrew Roots homeschool families. Melody and I therefore read dozens, if not hundreds, of children's books on biblical topics. Most of them were horrid. We would read them quickly; take notes on their style, accuracy, and value; and add the notes to a growing pile of note cards. It was informative in many ways, though I cannot strongly recommend it as a pastime.

Over one winter break when I was probably fourteen, my parents decided I was old enough to read *The Lord of the Rings*, something I had been eager to do since reading *The Hobbit* several years before. I devoured *The Fellowship of the Ring* in three days and *The Two Towers* in four. We then left home to spend a week at a family friend's cabin on a lake in Alabama, which significantly slowed my pace in reading *The Return of the King*. But the delay was worth it. The cabin made an impression, in part because it was a summer cabin. The weather was icy, the lake was forlorn, and the cabin was frigid. Even today, though I know that Mordor is supposed to be oppressively hot, I cannot help thinking of it as cold and drafty, like that cabin.

Tolkien led me to another encounter with Catholicism. I was so enthralled by this work of literature that my mother enrolled me in a summer course in Norse Mythology offered online through Regina Caeli Academy. The class did not leave a lasting impression, but in it I made my first online friends—and my first real Catholic friends.

This also happened during a painfully embarrassing time in my life: my teen years. I do not think I was an exceptional teenager; I was uncomfortable in my skin, trying to create an identity for myself, and making social blunders by sticking my foot in my mouth. Moreover, my generation had the great misfortune of doing much of this painfully embarrassing growing up on the internet, where the record was kept longer. I spent a lot of my youth saying boneheaded things on the internet, and I will save some face here by not repeating them. The internet provided me with an opportunity to hear the perspectives of intelligent and educated traditional Christians, mostly Protestant, and while I continued to disagree with their perspectives, which often lacked explanatory power regarding my questions on the Torah and the Messiah's relationship to it, I could no longer dismiss them as simply uneducated and completely misguided.

The internet stretched me a great deal. While Mom had always been a good conversation partner, I was now offered a wider range of views; and though most of them were not thought out as well as hers, they cracked open my very linear reasoning to alternatives that needed to be considered. I met my first convert from Christianity to Judaism, as well as my first atheists and New Age mystics.

The possibilities were endless—and overwhelming. It was at this stage that I underwent my great existential crisis, and I realized I needed to make sure I understood my beliefs and positions from the ground up. I wanted to base all my beliefs strictly on reason, and at the time, I thought that meant having no unjustified presuppositions. Nothing should be presupposed except what was self-evident, but that created an obvious problem: What was self-evident? Was self-evidence even possible? This question bothered me to an unsettling extent, and my earlier apocalyptically focused tendency toward the melancholy found a new center of anxiety: epistemic uncertainty.

One day while I was working on my geometry homework, an idea that I would later learn to formulate more philosophically occurred to me: while I could offer proofs concerning a triangle, there was no proof that the triangle *was* a triangle. In fact, the desire to have a logical proof for everything itself rested on an unprovable claim that logic should be the basis of my beliefs and philosophies. Any proof that I could attempt to offer in defense of reason and logic failed automatically because it appealed to logical categories and arguments, which was the logical fallacy of assuming the consequent. That is to say, the argument assumed a particular conclusion from the beginning, rather than proving it. Not only could I not prove reason, but I could not escape it because even absurdism was a rationalist argument from this inability of reason to justify itself. Absurdism was simply the conclusion that reason is the correct way of judging the truth of everything, including reason itself. Reason, in its broad, commonsense definition, was the water in which I swam, and no matter how I poked and prodded and attempted to circumvent it, there it stood as the unmoving logos. First Principles were exactly that—first, not asking or permitting any basis except faith. I did not know how near I was to Saint John's theology of the Word.

My sense of chronology is highly imperfect, and it may be that the next two events happened somewhat earlier in my youth—the first perhaps as early as age twelve and the second about thirteen. But I am trying to balance the logical progression of my thought processes, and therefore when information became important, with when the thought processes actually occurred, and so I do not think them out of place here, though my memory of the exact sequence of events is obscured.

In addition to my taking logic in high school, my mother introduced me to two short Socratic dialogues by Peter Kreeft that were influential in my thinking. They were *The Unaborted Socrates*, a narrowly focused discourse on abortion and when life begins, and *Between Heaven and Hell*, a wider-ranging discussion of the reasonableness of the basic doctrines of Christianity, especially the divinity of Christ and historicity of the Resurrection. The latter had a much greater impact on me and saved me from some of the more dangerous aspects of the Hebrew Roots Movement and Messianic Judaism that I would later encounter. It was the latest of God's prevenient interventions in my life through Catholics. Both the Socratic form of discourse and Kreeft's clear, concise, cutting style of argumentation stayed with me as a model to imitate, however poorly.

Kreeft is a philosopher by training and a professor of philosophy by trade, rather than an apologist or a theologian, and this is one of the great advantages of his books over others of their kind. In *Between Heaven and Hell*, he imagines a post-death meeting between C. S. Lewis, John F. Kennedy, and Aldous Huxley, who all died within a few hours of one another in 1963. In this book, Kennedy represents scientific materialism; Huxley, Eastern mysticism; and Lewis, Catholic Christianity. Kreeft's Lewis adopts a modified version of Lewis' "Lord, liar, or lunatic" argument for Christ: that because Jesus claims to be God, He must be a madman or a wicked man or what He says He is. Kreeft adds a fourth possibility: that He was misunderstood or misrepresented by His followers. Kreeft demonstrates concisely why three of the alternatives are unlikely: upon reading the accounts of Him, we all agree, more or less, that He was neither insane nor immoral; we also do not have historically viable evidence of another version of Jesus, and the Gospels present such a consistent characterization of the man that it is nonsensical to claim that He was invented or that the Gospel writers misrepresented Him. Therefore, Jesus must truly be the Lord: there is no other reasonable explanation of the evidence.

The second influence was introduced early but did not come to a head until I was fifteen or sixteen, had gained a certain facility with Hebrew, and was learning to do research. Michael Rood had noted a problem with the "Yeshua was a Karaite" thesis: in Matthew 23:2–3, Yeshua tells the crowd that because the scribes and Pharisees "sit in Moses' seat", the people should do whatever they tell them to do, but because of the scribes' and Pharisees' hypocrisy, the people should not imitate them. If Yeshua was a Karaite who rejected Pharisaic authority, why did he tell the crowd to do whatever the Pharisees said? Enter Nehemia Gordon.

Gordon proposed a solution based on another version of the Gospel of Matthew. In what follows, I will attempt to be fair to Mr. (now Dr.) Gordon's claims, but I have struggled to maintain a civil view of him in times since. First, a bit of background: We know that a Hebrew Gospel existed in antiquity for a very long time. In the fourth century, Saint Epiphanius of Salamis mentions the "Gospel of the Ebionites" or the "Gospel of the Nazoreans", referring to a Torah-observant Jewish-Christian sect known as the Ebionites or the Nazoreans and the only Gospel they accepted, written, according to Epiphanius, in "Hebrew".[1] Nearly everything about this is controversial. The only excerpts from it that definitely survive come to us in brief quotations in the commentaries of Saint Jerome, who is interested

[1] See Craig A. Evans, "The Jewish Christian Gospel Tradition", in *Jewish Believers in Jesus: The Early Centuries*, ed. Oskar Skarsaune and Reidar Hvalvik (Peabody, Mass.: Hendrickson Publishers, 2007), 250–53.

only in material not found in the canonical Gospels, so we have little idea of how similar it was to our Gospels.[2] It may have been merely a version of the Gospel of Saint Matthew, or it may have been a completely different Gospel in the Synoptic tradition. Even the identity of its language is controversial because what the New Testament calls "Hebrew" is, in fact, frequently Jewish Aramaic, as in John 19:17, where the name "Golgotha" is called "Hebrew" but is actually Aramaic. When Christ's words are given in Mark 5:41 and in Mark 15:34, they are in Aramaic, not Hebrew. Therefore, it may be that when Saint Epiphanius refers to a "Hebrew Gospel", he is referring to a Gospel written in Jewish Aramaic.

There is also a long tradition that, because the Gospel of Matthew was directed primarily at a Jewish audience, and a Galilean or Judean one at that, it may have been written in a Semitic language, either Hebrew or Aramaic. And while there are noticeable Semitisms in the Greek version of the first Gospel, the consensus is that it reads not like a translation but like an imitation of the Semitic style of the Greek Old Testament.[3]

Mr. Gordon pointed to the one Hebrew Gospel that has come down to us: a small number of copies of the Shem Tov Hebrew Matthew. This version of Saint Matthew's Gospel is written in biblical Hebrew style and exists in several manuscripts from the fourteenth and fifteenth centuries, connected with a Jewish countermissionary text by Rabbi Shem Tov ben Isaac. The editor of our main critical edition of this Gospel, George Howard, argued that it is, in fact, an ancient version and may be closer to the original

[2] Ibid., 253–58.

[3] For a Jewish perspective on this question, see Aaron M. Gale, "The Gospel according to Matthew", in *The Jewish Annotated New Testament*, ed. Amy-Jill Levine and Marc Zvi Brettler (New York: Oxford University Press, 2011), 1–2.

Gospel of Matthew than the Greek version is. It is important to note, however, that almost no one else agrees with Professor Howard. While there is some evidence that this version did not originate in the fifteenth century, when I obtained a copy of Howard's book through interlibrary loan, I discovered that he was able to trace its predecessors only to about the ninth century, and even then, the version showed significant change over time.[4]

Gordon went on to point out that in a minority of manuscripts of this Hebrew Matthew—in two out of ten, to be exact—23:3 reads, "Whatever they tell you to do, you shall not do and observe." This he latched on to as resolving what he perceived to be a problem in the characterization of Yeshua. Leaning heavily on his degree for authority, Mr. Gordon argued that this must be the original reading of Matthew 23:3 because it explains this difficulty.[5]

This was an incredibly appealing solution to an objection we had to this passage. And it seemed natural to accept it. But once I had read the actual evidence in Howard's critical edition of the book, it struck me as incredibly untenable. A family friend who lived and worked for the Baptist church in Israel, Mr. W——, pointed out that fifteen hundred years, or even nine hundred years, is a long time in terms of textual transmission, while our oldest manuscripts of this passage in Greek are from the third and fourth centuries. And even if the Shem Tov version is reliable to some extent, not only was this an extreme minority reading among its own manuscripts, but it destroyed the logical sequence of the chapter. What did it even mean to say, "The scribes and the Pharisees sit in Moses' seat: All therefore whatsoever they

[4] George Howard, *The Gospel of Matthew according to a Primitive Hebrew Text* (Macon, Ga.: Mercer University Press, 1987).

[5] See Nehemia Gordon, *The Hebrew Yeshua vs. the Greek Jesus: New Light on the Seat of Moses from Shem-Tov's Hebrew Matthew* (n.p.: Hilkiah Press, 2005).

bid you observe, that do not do; but do not ye after their works: for they say, and do not. For they bind heavy burdens and grievous to be borne, and lay them on men's shoulders; but they themselves will not move them with one of their fingers"? (23:2–4).

I preferred the more common Hebrew Roots interpretation, which took "Moses' seat" to refer to the place where the scroll of the Torah was read in the synagogue. In other words, "Do what they say" when they are reading from the Bible, "but do not do what they do"—that is, follow their application of those words in their own lives. This was also a strained interpretation, not least because the Torah was traditionally read not sitting down but standing; it was a better alternative, however, than this egregious distortion of evidence.

This debate introduced me to the world of textual criticism: the study of manuscripts and their differences. It was an exciting new prospect and field of research for me. In high school, I had very limited Greek and no Latin or Aramaic, but now I began delving into the study of textual difficulties, especially in the Old Testament. Around the same time, I began writing a weekly commentary on the Torah portion, which I would email to those who asked. It was not particularly popular because it concerned questions that I was interested in, rather than the kinds of mysteries and apocalypses that people were generally looking for. I believe my longest commentary was my attempt to understand what Genesis 49:22–26, a text with famously difficult grammar, was saying.

At this time, I did not read any sources explaining biblical manuscripts or textual criticism, and my grasp of the discipline was loose indeed. I understood only that there were different copies of the biblical books, that they did not always agree, and that we needed to use reason to understand which reading was oldest. Some of my conclusions from this period would later be justified, and some would prove hopelessly ill informed.

Disappointment regarding the Shem Tov Matthew was not the end of my study of Semitic-language versions of the New Testament. I soon learned there were two others that had some claim to antiquity. The first I learned about was the Peshitta, the Aramaic New Testament used by several churches in the Near East. The Peshitta is written in a dialect of Aramaic called Syriac, which originated in ancient Syria, an area spanning modern Syria and parts of Turkey, Lebanon, and Iraq. Many of the Christians who continue to use this version have become more familiar to Westerners in the wake of their persecution by the Islamic State during the Syrian civil war. Today there are communities of Syriac Christians in Lebanon, Iraq, and even southern India, but before the rise of Islam they used to stretch across Iran and Central Asia, reaching even China and Mongolia.

The history of the Syriac-speaking churches is long and complex and would take far too long to tell. What interested me as a young man was the discovery that some of their members, especially in the Assyrian Church of the East, believed that the Peshitta was actually the original version of the New Testament—having been written in Syriac before being translated into Greek. The first advocate of this position in the West was the odd character George Lamsa, who claimed that a Syriac original could explain the differences between Greek manuscripts of the New Testament because they were merely different translations of a single Aramaic original.[6]

The Peshitta had a major advantage over the Shem Tov in that we have fifth- and sixth-century copies of it and even

[6] See George M. Lamsa, *The Modern New Testament: From the Aramaic*, deluxe study edition, ed. Daniel Jon Mahar (Martinez, Ga.: Aramaic Bible Society, 2001), xv–xxiii.

earlier references to it. A Syriac version may date to the mid-third century, though that was likely more closely related to the Old Syriac Gospels found at Saint Catherine's in Sinai, a kind of precursor to the Peshitta. Not only was it ancient, but it was preserved and included—at least in some versions—the entire New Testament. I acquired three versions, two of them parallel English and Aramaic editions, and this became my standard New Testament until college. I spent hours poring over the Aramaic, a Syriac-English lexicon in hand, so that even though I never acquired a Syriac grammar, I gained a modest facility with the language.

The process was exciting and promised a more Jewish, more Semitic Jesus by nature of its language. I was involved in messaging boards to discuss "Bible codes" of dubious statistical validity, textual issues, and cultural revelations. But in the end, there was exceedingly little substance to these. The Peshitta community made bold claims, for instance, about how the Aramaic word *Mila*, "Word", in chapter 1 of John's Gospel indicated a deeper mystical and philosophical theology of the Word. However, I could not see anything here that we did not already know through the dual Greek associations of Logos found in philosophy and in the Septuagint: that the Word is the creative Word of God and also the logic of the universe, which He created.

In the midst of my discovery of the Peshitta, my family made our first pilgrimage to the Holy Land. The land of Israel had been built up in our imaginations over the preceding four years to an exceedingly high degree. Mr. R—— regaled us with stories about the moment when a person finds the special place in Israel that marks his heritage and of how he broke down sobbing when he found his. I do not know how our visit could have been anything but a disappointment after all the hype.

We went in the off-season to save costs and connected with our friend Mr. W——, previously mentioned, who worked and lived in Israel. He met us at the airport in Tel Aviv, and to keep us from dozing off due to jet lag, he took us directly to explore Mount Carmel. Our first breath of open air in Israel was atop a lookout point over the Jezreel Valley, a matter of yards from the ancient holy site of the Cave of Elijah, on the mountain of the prophet's confrontation with the priests of Baal. And I felt absolutely nothing. Do not misunderstand me; the gravity of the location was completely impressed on my mind, and I had an aesthetic appreciation of the truly beautiful green fertile valley that stretched below, but no more than I would have if it had been any lovely green valley in Pennsylvania. It was a letdown that I had not expected. The sun beat down on us for almost the only time during that entire trip; the valley was rich and thick with crops, but I felt completely hollow.

From there, we pressed on to our host's home in the city of Haifa, at the mouth of the Jezreel Valley, which separates Samaria southward from Galilee to the north. We arrived just in time for the festival of Purim, which we celebrated with our hosts, the W—— family, and their Jewish-Christian congregation in Haifa. Purim is not one of the seven feasts and fasts commanded in Leviticus 23, but it is the celebration of God's deliverance of the Jewish people through Esther under the Persian Empire. It is traditionally celebrated by a dramatic reading of the entire Book of Esther, dressing in costumes, and eating filled cookies called *hamantaschen*, that is, "Haman's hats" or "Haman's ears", after the villain in Esther.

Purim was something of a conundrum for the Hebrew Roots community because we were opposed to traditions that were not part of the Law expressly given by God; the

Bible did not seem to share our scruples, however, and included a feast in the liturgical calendar whose origin came a thousand years after Moses' revelation on Mount Sinai. In fact, Esther 9:26–28 indicated that the Jewish people had taken this holiday upon themselves as a binding obligation, not merely an optional celebration—precisely the kind of traditional addition to the Torah that we opposed on principle! We typically shrugged our shoulders and said it was clearly in the Bible, so there could not be anything wrong with celebrating it, but it was not, strictly speaking, a requirement. And we carried on celebrating it.

6

Our first trip to Israel was interesting and informative and, in some ways, remarkable. We spent most of our time in the north because our base was in Haifa, and we traveled to Nazareth, Caesarea Maritima, Beth Shean, Tiberias, Tel Dan, and the Golan Heights. We assiduously avoided traditional Christian sites, which we viewed as inherently unreliable, but we admired places such as Nazareth in general terms. Mr. W—— explained to us that there are three tiers of biblical sites in Israel: (1) places where the events in the Bible are established to have taken place, (2) places where biblical events are reasonably assumed to have taken place, though it is hard to confirm, and (3) sites that are traditional but historically nonsensical. I would continue to say there is some truth to these categories, though I would now dispute which sites belong in the third category.

Galilee and the Jezreel Valley were beautiful and helped me get a firmer grip on the stories that I read in the Bible, especially the New Testament. To a Texan, the tiny scale of the Holy Land was itself a revelation, and it may have given rise to my love of little places, of little lands. Israel was cozy in a way that the vast, unending plains of West Texas are not. One could see from the head of the Jezreel all the way to the sea on a clear day, but Christ had lived His entire life and died more or less in this homey corner at the junction of three wide continents.

In the second half of our journey, we drove through the Negev wilderness and saw an elaborate replica of the tabernacle in Timna Park, spent one night on the Gulf of Aqaba at Eilat, and then entered Jerusalem from the east after visiting Ein Gedi, Qumran, and Masada on our return north. This was the Middle East I had come expecting: great rock-and-sand deserts and scrub-encrusted hills. It was dramatic and romantic, and the score of *Lawrence of Arabia* played itself in all our minds as we shot across the molten-gold Ramon Crater in a poorly air-conditioned rental car.

Jerusalem was also an emotional disappointment. I liked the city, the holy sites, the culture, and the food. It snowed while we were there, which was a rare and beautiful treat, though it melted almost immediately and Melody ended up soaked to the waist when a passing car sprayed her and Mr. W——'s daughter with snowmelt. But I had no epiphany, and my feeling of home-longing only intensified because the Holy Land, which was supposed to feel like home, felt only like another foreign place. The alienation that I felt in Midland I also felt in Jerusalem.

More compelling was the availability of kosher food, the ease of observing the Sabbath, and the ubiquitous books and materials for Torah observance. I was delighted by Jerusalem in a way reminiscent of how I was delighted by Denver as a boy—because one never ceased to discover little bookshops, whether centrally and prominently located or tucked away in some nook behind a barely noticeable archway. The cobbles and walls and packed streets of the Old City offered a completely different kind of antiquity from the windswept hilltop ruins of Galilee and the Jezreel: it was a living, breathing antiquity. I did not understand at the time that I was experiencing not a pure ancient Israel but the developments of medieval Palestine: the Crusader churches and Ottoman edifices, with bazaars and hangings and hookas and Turkish coffee. It was a continuous and growing tradition that came from antiquity through the medieval era and on down to modernity, with both continuity and growth and change, as in all living cultures. It was an experience, and an exciting one taken on its own cultural grounds. But it was not the one I had come seeking.

In Jerusalem, I purchased a set of *tefillin* for myself, marking a turning point in my relationship with Jewish tradition. Tefillin, or phylacteries, as they are called in the New Testament, are black leather boxes containing scrolls with texts from Exodus and Deuteronomy that are bound to the forehead and the left bicep during morning and afternoon prayers. This is done in accord with a literal interpretation of the commandment in Deuteronomy 6:8 to "bind [these words] for a sign upon thine hand and ... as frontlets between thine eyes". Interestingly, the Karaites have typically taken this as figurative language, referring to how the Jewish people should keep God's laws in their minds and deeds at all times, rather than physically wearing them. Someone pointed out to me, however, that in Matthew 23:5, the Messiah criticizes the Pharisees' use of phylacteries only for making them big and showy, not for using them in the first place. Furthermore, this is coupled with a criticism for making tzitziot, the fringes discussed earlier, too long, but we all agreed that their use was commanded literally (see Num 15:38–39).

My adoption of this practice was only one manifestation of my growing love and longing for ritual. Despite our adoption of the "ritual law", our community had retained a kind of Protestant resistance to formal rites and ceremonies. We performed circumcision, ritual purification, and meal blessings with as little ceremony as possible. But a growing familiarity with Jewish life and practice uncovered a desire I did not previously know I had: to engage in ritual, to make it a part of my life—in fact, to form my life around it.

Even before my family's trip to Israel, we had begun using traditional Jewish blessings over our food and incorporating other elements of traditional ritual, including Sabbath candles on Friday nights and the *Haggadah*, the book of ritual for the Passover Seder. Through mere contact with the Jewish tradition, it became abundantly clear why ritual was valuable: it taught us, it formed virtuous habits in us, and, more than that, it opened our vision to a wider view, to an encounter that was luminous and ineffable. I could give you certain theological reasons why ritual forms this connection, but in the end, I cannot tell you because it is not a reason but an experience. The flickering Sabbath lights in the darkness are their own explanation, and they require no other. I will say further only that the experience is akin to the awe of standing in front of a great work of art in its intended setting in a church or a palace, rather than the antithesis of seeing it in a sterile museum. Our trip to Israel cemented that desire in me, culminating in my purchase of the tefillin, which then required the adoption of a whole set of rituals in prayer that I had not followed before.

About this time, but before our trip, I had begun working on a prayer book. The Bible made it abundantly clear to me that certain prayers were commanded, especially the texts that traditionally make up the Shema—that is, Deuteronomy 6:4–9; 11:13–21 and Numbers 15:37–41—and the Lord's Prayer. These passages themselves said they should be recited either "when thou liest down, and when thou risest up" (Deut 6:7) or "when thou prayest" (Mt 6:5). Additionally, I returned to the psalms, understanding them as the prayers of Israel that must have been intended to accompany these commanded prayers as well as the sacrifices in the Temple.

I assumed that each psalm had been composed for a particular holy day or time or sacrifice, so I began working to identify which psalms were intended to accompany which days, which hours of prayer, and which festivals. There is a clear Sabbath psalm, which is prefaced "A psalm, a song for the Sabbath" (Ps 92), an obvious prayer for accompanying or replacing the evening sacrifice (Ps 141), and psalms that tell the story of the Exodus and must have been intended for the Passover Seder, when it was commanded that we recount the events related to the festival (Ps 78; 136; Ex 13:3, 14–16). My prayer book had only two Daily Offices, morning and evening, and each was very short, consisting of only the prayers I could find prescribed in the Bible, with the addition of one psalm at each, or two on Sabbaths and festivals. When I began using tefillin, I added the blessings that traditionally accompanied tying them on. There was a strange incongruity between the traditional, almost institutional, leather strap I wrapped around my arm and the homemade prayer book written on 8½-by-11-inch paper, from which I prayed that first night at the dining table of a poorly lit attic apartment in the New City of Jerusalem. This was the beginning of a movement in a new direction, but first I must address the problem of the liturgical calendar.

As I alluded to earlier, the calendar in Leviticus 23 is divided neatly into two holy seasons. The first is in the spring, consisting of the feasts of Passover and Unleavened Bread, with the minor festival of Firstfruits happening midweek in the feast of Unleavened Bread, followed seven weeks later by the feast of Weeks known as Shavuot in Hebrew and Pentecost in Greek. The second season is in the fall, seven months after Passover, beginning with the feast of Trumpets, known as Jewish New Year or Rosh Hashanah, followed by Yom Kippur, the Day of Atonement, ten days later, and culminating in the feast of Tabernacles, Sukkot, which lasts for seven days and is immediately followed by the concluding celebration of the eighth great day, Shemini Atzeret. There is also the later festival of Purim in February or March and Hanukkah, which is not mentioned in the Hebrew Bible because it celebrates the victory of the Maccabees, a story not found in the Hebrew Bible. Jewish tradition also includes in late summer a feast called *Tisha-b'Av*, commemorating the destruction of the Temple, and, shortly after midwinter, a New Year for trees, called *Tu BiShvat*.

It may be surprising that nearly every aspect of this calendar was controversial among Hebrew Roots believers. We were divided over whether to celebrate Hanukkah, though most chose to celebrate it because the New Testament suggests in John 10:22 that the Messiah did so. This in itself created controversy, which I will discuss soon. But the problem went deeper.

First of all, the Bible does not detail how the calendar is calculated. It is clear that the calendar is lunisolar, taking into account both the lunar cycle, on which the months are based, and the solar cycle, on which the year is based. The beginning of each month[1] is celebrated when the new moon is sighted, and based on that sighting, the dates of festivals are calculated as the first, tenth, or fifteenth day of the month. The festivals are also matched to the agricultural seasons, which means taking the sun into account. But the Bible does not make explicit how the calendar is to be aligned with the solar cycle or what counts as a "new moon".

In a fascinating twist, both the mainstream of rabbinic tradition and the Karaites essentially agree on how this was done in ancient times. Rather than making complex

[1] The historical meaning of the English word "month" is literally "moon"-th, and the same is true of the Hebrew, where the word *hodesh* means "new", referring to the new moon.

calculations based on the celestial cycles, the Israelites, who, unlike their Babylonian neighbors, did not develop complex astronomy until later, observed the plant life of Judea and Jerusalem to determine when spring had come. A special emphasis was placed on the ripeness of the barley crop because the Bible states that Passover takes place in the month of "Abib" (Deut 16:1), which refers to a certain stage of development in the grains of barley. The readiness of the barley was all the more significant for this timing because during the week of Unleavened Bread, on the feast of Firstfruits, Israel was commanded to wave a sheaf of newly harvested barley before God in the Temple (see Lev 23:10–11), indicating that Passover could not be celebrated until the barley harvest was beginning. So, if the twelfth new moon came and went and the barley was not ready to harvest, a leap month was added to give it time to mature, which had the effect of keeping the lunar and solar calendars aligned.

Not everyone in the ancient Jewish world agreed, though. The sectarians at Qumran and the author of the Book of Enoch used a different, more mathematical calendar. In the Book of Enoch, the year is 364 days with no exceptions, causing an inevitable drift away from the solar cycle. It also does not use the new moon to begin the month but, rather, divides the year into arbitrary months of 30 or 31 days, like the Julian and Gregorian calendars that we use today. A slightly modified version of this calendar was used by the Qumran community, which gave us the Dead Sea Scrolls, though they may have had some kind of recourse for correcting the calendar to match the solar year.[2]

[2] See Robert Eisenman and Michael Wise, *The Dead Sea Scrolls Uncovered* (New York: Barnes and Noble Books, 1992), 106–9.

Although there were other calendars used by other Jewish communities in the ancient world, these were the ones mostly discussed. After the Bar Kokhba Revolt in A.D. 132–137, the Jewish people were forbidden to live in Jerusalem and were generally exiled from Judea, which created a problem for the calendar. You see, the observation of the new moons and the ripe barley were regarded as specific to the Holy Land, especially Jerusalem and Judea, and exile from there meant it was not possible to observe the calendar as it was meant to be observed. As a result, the ancient method was gradually replaced by a more complex mathematical calendar with regularly recurring leap years, though it is still the practice to add a whole leap month, rather than a leap day, as became standard in our Roman calendar. This system was basically in place by the mid-fourth century, but it continued to be corrected in minor ways.

The basic controversy that arose among members of the Hebrew Roots Movement was whether to follow common Jewish practice and use the mathematical calendar, which even the Karaites had done as a result of the exile, or, because the Jewish people had a home in the Holy Land again, to return to the ancient use, as many modern Karaites have. Because disputes frequently arose over what qualified as the *abib* stage of maturation in barley, and whether the barley had reached that stage in any given year, the traditional calendar was more reliable. Sometimes even the Karaites would end up celebrating Passover at different times, depending on their individual or local judgment. The traditionalist argument was that without a functioning Temple and priesthood, and without an established Sanhedrin (the high court of Israel) to decide cases like this, it was impossible to return to the ancient calendar. As you can imagine, this was a deeply unsatisfactory argument to a lot of libertarian-minded former Baptists, but neither was it satisfactory for everyone to celebrate the same feasts but not be able to celebrate them together. It led inevitably to fracturing along calendrical lines, despite a desire for community. Upon our return to Texas, the contrast with our time in Israel could not have been starker.

To make matters worse, there were factions of the community that adopted other calendars. No one in our area adopted the calendar from the Book of Enoch, which was obviously unworkable, but there was a wide range of theories and proposals. One that began to gain traction a little later was the idea of a "lunar Sabbath" calendar, which posited that the week was not independent of the lunar month but that each month began on the first day of the week, and the month then divided neatly into four weeks, each of which corresponded to one quarter of the moon, with two or three extra days of new-moon celebration when the moon was dark. Then there was the controversy over whether "new moon" referred to the dark of the moon or to the appearance of its first new sliver.

Without any tradition and no source of unifying authority, it became clear that there was no way to reach consensus. Some were even accused of changing the calendar they used each year, adopting whichever one had the most feast days that fell on weekends, in order to avoid taking days off from work. One year, the Karaites in Israel, on whom we relied for information about the new moon and the abib barley, disagreed with some of our local farmers about whether the barley was sufficiently developed; this led to a fracture among the largest group of those who followed the Abib calendar. It was our clearest indication that not all was well in this system, that our individual decisions and conclusions affected the whole community, and that without some kind of arbiter we were never going to have a meaningful community; however, nobody was willing to submit to anyone else as an authority. Most of us fell back on the traditional calendar as less controversial rather than appealing to someone as the source of the decisions about new moons and abib barley.

Part of our more nuanced stance regarding Jewish tradition was the result of an expanding familiarity with both antiquity and the classical Karaites. While in high school, I ordered a copy of Leon Nemoy's excellent *Karaite Anthology* from the Yale Judaica Series. Many of the medieval Karaite scholars evinced no objection to traditions associated with the Oral Torah, as long as they did not expressly contradict what was in the written Torah.[3] In fact, such traditions could be helpful in situations like the one we were facing regarding the calendar. This seemed to be the position of Yeshua in the Gospels as well, who, in Matthew 23:23, did not object absolutely to the oral tradition of tithing "mint and anise and cummin" but objected to prioritizing it over the "weightier matters" of the Torah.

But many did not share our concern for unity, despite Scripture's clear focus on it: "Behold how good and how pleasant it is for brethren to dwell together in unity!", writes the psalmist (133:1). Saint Paul encourages us to endeavor "to keep the unity of the Spirit in the bond of peace"

[3] In the words of the fifteenth-century Karaite scholar Elijah Bashyatchi, "Karaite tradition ... is such as is acknowledged by all Israel, and it does not stand up against that which is recorded in the Writ of divine truth; and our scholars have said that every tradition which does not stand up against Scripture, does not add to what is stated in Scripture, is acknowledged by all Israel, and has indirect support in Scripture, is to be called genuine tradition, and we must accept it. They said further that most of the Mishnah and the Talmud comprises genuine utterances of our forefathers, and Rabbi Nissin ben Noah has said that our people are obligated to study the Mishnah and Talmud." Leon Nemoy, ed., *Karaite Anthology: Excerpts from the Early Literature* (New Haven: Yale University Press, 1952), 249–50.

(Eph 4:3). And Yeshua prays that His followers "may be one" as He and the Father are one (Jn 17:22). The inability of a large part of the community to relinquish private interpretation in the interest of unity struck a serious blow to my family's confidence in the project of a Karaite-inspired Hebrew Roots Movement. On a basic, practical level, unity was impossible without some tradition and authority.

The *Karaite Anthology* introduced me to a new interest: obscure and ancient sects. I continued refusing to study rabbinic texts and theology, but I dove headfirst into every other obscure form of Jewish or Israelite practice and tradition. I read the Dead Sea Scrolls exhaustively in Geza Vermes' translation. I acquired *Tradition Kept: The Literature of the Samaritans* by Robert T. Anderson and Terry Giles, which concerns the fascinating Samaritan community that has existed since the time of Ezra and continues, though greatly reduced, to this day. I also bought Wolf Leslau's *Falasha Anthology*, the Yale Judaica Series volume on Ethiopian Jewry and their unique, ancient traditions, including books of the Bible such as Enoch that are not considered canonical elsewhere and mystical texts on the Sabbath. These other Judaisms revealed very clearly a set of traditional interpretations that differed from those of mainstream Judaism and seemed to frustrate, to a certain extent, the Karaite view that if one left behind rabbinic material, the interpretation of the Torah became relatively clear. The norm was to have an interpretive tradition, and it was absolutely necessary to the community's survival.

I read very little of Philo of Alexandria because, though he was ancient, he stank of the "Hellenism" with which we indicted traditional Christianity, traditional Judaism, and anyone with whom we disagreed. The Greeks were, as far as we were concerned, the source of all paganism. And to a certain extent, we were right about Philo: his project was to make Judaism compatible with the Platonic philosophy of his Greek contemporaries.[4]

Once again, I was in the midst of mysteries. I felt I was learning secrets that only the wise knew and that the answers to our questions about interpretation and application were in these mysterious sects. We needed to embrace our own ancient tradition, which was delivered to us by Yeshua and His disciples in the form of the New Testament. We needed to treat the Gospels and Epistles as our Mishnah and Talmud, the most important compendia of Jewish tradition. When we talked about interpretation and application of the Torah, we needed to treat Yeshua as our great Rabbi and take seriously into consideration both the actual rulings that He seemed to make on specific issues and His method of approach in order to learn the rules for interpreting the Torah. I did not see this being widely or systematically done by those around me at the time, not in the way that I was reading about in Philo or the Karaites. Yeshua was typically treated as simply a member of one existing school or another: Michael Rood considered Him a Sadducee, while others, such as Ron Moseley, treated Him as simply a Pharisee of the school of the first-century rabbi Hillel.[5]

Despite the calendar controversy, I remember this as, in many ways, a very rich time. I was discovering a wealth of tradition and culture and felt, in some ways, immersed. My family read Jewish literature, such as works by Chaim Potok and Milton Steinberg; listened to Jewish music by such artists as Neshama Carlebach, Moshav Band, Blue

[4] See David M. Scholer, "An Introduction to Philo Judaeus of Alexandria", foreword to C.D. Yonge, *The Works of Philo: Complete and Unabridged*, new updated edition (Peabody, Ma.: Hendrickson Publishers, 1992), xi–xviii.

[5] See Dr. Ron Moseley, *Yeshua: A Guide to the Real Jesus and the Original Church* (Clarksville, Md.: Messianic Jewish Publishers, 1998).

Fringe, and Matisyahu; listened to Jewish stories, such as the enchanting family tales of Laura Pershin Raynor; and watched Jewish movies, such as *Ushpizin*, *Yentl*, and *Fiddler on the Roof.* My mother rightly saw that the Torah was more than a legal code; it was a way of life, a culture, so it was essential that we immerse ourselves in that culture. But while I felt a sense of pride in this culture, which I claimed belonged to me by right through the Messiah, it was at the same time deeply alienating because I knew that, in all material senses, I did not belong to it and was not accepted by it.

These two things combined—delving into ancient Jewish and Samaritan traditions with an eye to interpreting the Torah and entering into Jewish culture despite resisting the authority of its tradition—enriched our reading of the Bible. Up to this time, we had continued to read the Bible essentially the way we did as Baptists, seeking only one grammatical and historical meaning. Now we began to appreciate the fourfold method of traditional Judaism, which interpreted Scripture as *peshat*—the plain, literal meaning; *remez*—the hidden or allegorical meaning; *drash*—the hidden reference, independent of context; and *sod*—the mystical, esoteric meaning about the nature of God and encountering Him.[6] The flat world of Scripture suddenly acquired depth. "I stand alone on the word of God" became "And many people shall go and say, Come ye, and let us go up to the mountain of the LORD, to the house of the God of Jacob; and he will teach us of his ways, and we will walk in his paths: for out of Zion shall go forth the law, and the word of the LORD from Jerusalem" (Is 2:3).

[6] See Benjamin Edidin Scolnic, "Traditional Methods of Bible Study", in *Etz Hayim: Torah and Commentary*, ed. David L. Lieber (New York: Jewish Publication Society, 2001), 1494–99.

These traditions of reading the Bible, with the exception of the Karaites', took it for granted that the Bible is a multilayered text. It did not yield all of its secrets easily but required that one invest himself, that he live the tradition, that he give himself over wholly to the text and to its study. David Lyle Jeffrey describes this as allowing yourself to "be read by the text".[7] Even the New Testament seemed to assume this approach because its quotations of the Old Testament were elliptical and its interpretation of them was indirect and suggested secret meanings. When the prophet Hosea talks about God's calling the nation of Israel out of Egypt in 11:1, Matthew insists that this refers to the Messiah (2:15). That was not a surface-level meaning; it was more akin to a remez or a drash, which did not read the words merely for what they appeared to mean but penetrated them to some kind of secret level that I did not fully understand.

Jewish tradition became for us not a requirement or a source of law but a reference for enrichment. The Torah commanded that we recite the Shema, and Judaism enriched it by adding the *Baruch shem kavod malkhuto l'olam va'ed*: "Blessed be the name of His glorious kingdom forever and again." The Torah commanded that we tell the story of the Exodus at Passover, and Judaism enriched it by letting a drop of wine drip from the teller's finger for each plague.[8] The world had warmth and depth and an aroma of incense because these traditions, this encircling culture, made the dead letter a living tradition.

[7] David Lyle Jeffrey, *People of the Book: Christian Identity and Literary Culture* (Grand Rapids, Mich.: William B. Eerdmans with the Institute for Advanced Christian Studies, 1996), 167–207.

[8] See Reuven Hammer, *Entering Jewish Prayer: A Guide to Personal Devotion and the Worship Service* (New York: Schocken Books, 1994), 121–22.

7

Committed as I was to finding a uniquely Messiah-centered version of the legal tradition, I returned to the sources. I had encountered Jewish Christians in the New Testament and in Eusebius, but I wanted to make a more careful study of these people to whom we were always appealing without much information. This required a little effort, though.

Mom drove me to the library of her alma mater, Hardin-Simmons University, three hours across the arid Southern Plains, to help me find a copy of Ray Pritz's *Nazarene Jewish Christianity*, which outlines the story of the ancient sects of the Nazarenes and the Ebionites. Briefly, the Nazarenes, mentioned in both Jewish and Christian sources, were Jewish Christians from the first four Christian centuries who fell into two categories: the Nazarenes proper, who believed that Yeshua was born of a virgin and who accepted the Gospel of the Hebrews, treated Saint James as their founder, and taught that all followers of the Messiah must be circumcised; and the Ebionites, who practiced the same but denied the Virgin Birth. Their writings have not survived intact, and they disappear after one reference to them by Saint Augustine in the early fifth century. Our sources also indicate that they observed the Torah "after the Jewish manner"—that is, according to the oral tradition.[1]

[1] Ray Pritz, *Nazarene Jewish Christianity: From the End of the New Testament Period until Its Disappearance in the Fourth Century* (Jerusalem: Magnes Press, 1992), 11–18, 21, 30–35.

In addition to historical mentions of the Nazarenes and the Ebionites, there is evidence that the earliest Christian liturgical text, the *Didache*, has some connection with ancient Jewish Christian groups.[2] We were fond of claiming that it was absolutely a Nazarene text, but that is more disputable. The *Didache* is a manual for Christian life and practice dating to the second century, focusing on the Ten Commandments, tithing, and the discerning and treatment of traveling prophets. It also contains the oldest ritual for celebrating a Christian ceremonial meal that survives outside the New Testament. There is a short blessing over the wine, a longer blessing over the bread dealing primarily with the gathering of the Church into one body, followed by a much longer blessing after the meal. As did many others in the Hebrew Roots Movement, I took this up immediately as belonging to us, but for what purpose was significantly less clear. We did not have a weekly celebration of Communion, though there is a ceremony connected to ushering in the Sabbath on Friday night by blessing bread and wine. But the main commemoration of the Paschal feast for us was, of course, the Paschal feast on Passover. In many ways, the blessings of the *Didache* were more satisfactory for the former, but I was rather desperate for them to be so for the latter, as an answer to the Christian celebration of Communion.

Actually employing anything like this in our community was always complicated, though. If we were celebrating Passover with friends, there was a good chance they were going to resist elaborate liturgy. I am also not known for planning ahead, and the liturgical choice typically went

[2] Anders Ekenberg, "Evidence for Jewish Believers in 'Church Orders' and Liturgical Texts", in *Jewish Believers in Jesus: The Early Centuries*, ed. Oskar Skarsaune and Reidar Hvalvik (Peabody, Ma.: Hendrickson Publishers, 2007), 640–58.

to the person who brought printouts. Because of these factors, I made very little actual use of the *Didache*'s blessings, but I was attached thenceforward because the book seemed to be exactly what I was looking for. I thought perhaps this was the key, the Messianic Mishnah, the secret to our ability to interpret the Bible. It would give us a method, so I studied it devotionally like the Bible or the Talmud.

On one trip to visit friends in South Carolina, perhaps in 2004 or 2005, we encountered our first true Messianic synagogue. There were people with Jewish heritage in our circles in Midland, but they had not grown up in observant Jewish families, and most of them were from families that had been practicing Christianity for generations. The community we visited in Charleston was very different from these friends, and they introduced us to the historic Messianic movement. They bore no grudges against Christianity; in fact, they considered themselves Christians. They were theologically orthodox Evangelicals who simply believed that their Jewish identity had a place in their Christian practice. It was a strange experience: our first time back in a traditional congregation that had its own building and did not divorce itself from the Christian mainstream. There was even a potluck afterward in the little kitchen in the back and creaky floorboards and musty smells like a small, older Baptist church.

The Hebrew Christian or Messianic Jewish movement has its roots in the nineteenth century, when it began as a joint effort between some Protestant leadership and Jewish converts to Christianity to create a space for Jews converting to maintain their heritage by baptizing it. This movement was founded on Saint Paul's principle stated in Romans 11:15, that if the casting away of the unbelieving Jews made way for the Gentiles, then what would their reconciliation be but life from the dead? The reconciliation of the Jewish people, as Jews, was desirable. And so, following in that legacy, the service of this congregation was an interesting mixture of traditional Jewish liturgy and Evangelical praise-and-worship music. The accoutrements were Jewish, but the theology was Christian. It was another strange and alienating experience, and it was also my first encounter with the work of Rabbi Dr. John Fischer.

Rabbi Fischer arranged and published the first practical prayer book, *Siddur* in Hebrew, for Messianic Jews. About the time of this trip, we acquired a copy of his Siddur, though I did not begin to use it seriously or completely until later. Like the services at the Messianic synagogue, it included most of the major traditional prayers of Judaism, but it added the Lord's Prayer and the Magnificat and the Pauline hymns, all in parallel Hebrew and English. I was not yet ready to acquiesce that much to Jewish tradition. I appreciated tradition, but still only as a resource to be used or plundered at will, and Rabbi Fischer seemed to me to be too liberal in his use of it.

I am afraid that much of this has been jumbled and I have not given enough dates, but the truth is that, for the most part, I do not know them. These last events happened when I was between fifteen and sixteen, during the years 2004 to 2006. It is difficult to know how to proceed from here, in part because the whole period was one of rapid change and very little stability. One friend in the Hebrew Roots Movement used to ask people, "How long have you been studying?"—meaning, "How long have you been involved in the movement?" That encapsulated our attitude toward many things. We were studying. We were always changing because we were always learning new information, and it kept us from achieving much in the way of stability.

Sometime in high school, I discovered the work of Geza Vermes on the "quest for the Historical Jesus", one of the successive attempts to parse out the relationship between the "Christ of faith" and the "Jesus of history". Vermes' books concentrate on the Jewishness of Jesus and were therefore appealing to me. In *Jesus the Jew*, *The Judaism of Jesus*, and *Jesus and the World of Judaism*, Vermes carefully works to place Jesus in His first-century Jewish setting. While these books were already somewhat outdated when I read them, they remain a testament to an important stage in Jesus scholarship in the latter twentieth century, and Vermes' accomplishment should not be underestimated. Though I have not read them since high school, as I remember it, Vermes saw Jesus as a largely mainstream Jewish teacher of the period, one of many miracle-workers with a broadly Pharisaic view on the Torah. He identifies Him with itinerant miracle-workers of the period known as *Hasidim*, "the Devout", revered by the rabbis and their predecessors, the Pharisees, but held with a degree of suspicion at the same time.[3]

The tension between rabbinic tradition and this charismatic Judaism that seemed more like Yeshua was highlighted particularly well in Vermes' work. The rabbinic authorities did not admit even divine intervention into legal discussions, which were based purely on tradition, precedent, and reason. To quote Vermes:

> Nowhere is this better illustrated than in the legendary account of a doctrinal argument around the end of the first century AD between Rabbi Eliezer ben Hyrcanus and his colleagues. Having exhausted his arsenal of reasoning and still not convinced them, he performed a miracle, only to

[3] Geza Vermes, *Jesus the Jew: A Historian's Reading of the Gospels* (Philadelphia: Fortress Press, 1981), 80–82.

> be told that there is no room for miracles in a legal debate. In exasperation he then exclaimed: "If my teaching is correct, may it be proved by Heaven!" Whereupon a celestial voice declared: "What have you against Rabbi Eliezer, for his teaching is correct?" But this intervention was ruled out of order because in the Bible it is written that decisions are to be reached by majority vote.[4]

Vermes offered a serious challenge to my Karaite understanding of the Messiah. What I took from Vermes, however, was not that the Jewish tradition that came down to us was entirely reliable but that it was a real, though imperfect and corrupted, descendant of the tradition that the Messiah belonged to. I began to take the tradition a little more seriously, but still not as a wholly reliable authority. It was venerable and worthy of consideration, perhaps, but the fact that Yeshua had critiques for the Pharisees writ large and for their use of the tradition, like these Hasidim in Vermes' books, made it clear that they at least falsely prioritized it and sometimes misinterpreted or manipulated it.

Two other influences were important at this time and need mention: Beit HaDerekh and Beged Ivri. About a twenty-minute drive from Midland stands her sister city of similar size, Odessa. You may be familiar with Odessa as the setting of the film *Friday Night Lights*. In between the cities is a modest charismatic church, whose fellowship hall was host every Saturday morning to the local Messianic congregation, Beit HaDerekh, meaning "House of the Way".

Beit HaDerekh is an interesting place, made up of a fascinating collection of people. It contains a combination of strict adherents to the Oral Torah and more charismatically

[4] Ibid., 81–82.

oriented families who at the very least do not treat the tradition as an authority. The services have continued to be much as they were when we first attended: they begin with a long "praise and worship" service of popular Messianic and Hebrew Roots songs (songs in a minor key that sprinkle Hebrew vocabulary throughout) sometimes interspersed with prayer and prophecy, while, off to one side, a group of women and some men perform Israeli folk dances. The music is followed by the only portion that has significantly changed: a brief liturgy, which has since expanded, made up of key texts of Jewish liturgy; a procession of the Torah scroll through the congregation, accompanied by dance and kissing the scroll covering (to "taste and see" that the Torah is sweet); then readings, mostly in English with some in Hebrew; and finally, the "teaching", which is what we insisted on calling our sermons, lest we be mistaken for Christians. At the time, there were two regular teachers, though others occasionally took a turn. I forget the name of one because he eventually left, taking many congregants with him. The other regular teacher was a young man, newly married at the time, named Ben.

Ben was different from the rest of us. He was already deeply committed to Jewish tradition and the Oral Torah, but he was much more interested in the study of Jewish mysticism, Kabbalah. He is a smart man and values intelligence above all other virtues. He wanted to connect Kabbalah to the theology of the Messiah—of who He was and what He came to do. I have quipped that Ben had only one sermon, which started with the Torah portion as a pretext to talk about one of the "divine attributes" and inevitably became a discussion about the ten attributes or emanations of God known as the *Sefirot* and how they relate to the Christian Trinity and the divinity of the Messiah. It then moved on to how that idea corresponds to the angel

Metatron, who is another part of the Divine. It is, of course, an unfair reduction, but I think Ben could see the humor and take his licks. He was the only one of us, at the time, who wore a proper *tallit katan*, the four-cornered garment worn under the day-to-day clothes on which the tzitziot, the ritual fringes, are tied.

For most of my youth, we did not strictly belong to any of the groups around us. We often attended a couple of the home fellowships and intermittently attended Beit HaDerekh. We rarely spent a week at home without going to one or another, but we did not settle in at any of them. Beit HaDerekh became particularly important for two reasons: First, it was the most organized, had a regular location to use, and eventually built its own building. Second, Ben and his erudition were recognized and widely appreciated and so became a draw: he was regularly invited to be a guest on the television station I have mentioned, God's Learning Channel, and drew to himself the Messianics interested in Orthodox Jewish tradition. And though we did not commit, we were drawn to that community, in large part because of Ben.

But Beit HaDerekh is also a prime example of the difficulty we faced as we began to appreciate traditional Judaism. At the time, many of us were still keeping only approximately kosher, or what some called "ingredient kosher"—that is, we did not eat anything that actually contained pork, but we were careless about packaged foods that were not checked by a rabbinic authority and restaurants that served unkosher food. Furthermore, on the basis of Exodus 23:19, "Thou shalt not seethe a kid in his mother's milk", Jewish tradition forbids eating meat and dairy together, but many of us continued to take this command at face value, saying it referred to a forbidden pagan practice, not a dietary law, strictly speaking.

A centrally important part of our community life, though, was the communal meal, which at Beit HaDerekh took the form of the traditional *oneg* meal after the service. When we were all providing food, how were those who kept a strict, Orthodox interpretation of kashrut supposed to eat with those who did not? If there were to be rules, who was going to make and impose them? Especially confounding was the fact that for those interested in the higher standard, this had implications for the cleanness of the vessels used and, in the Orthodox tradition, even the table surface or tablecloth! It remained a problem throughout my time there, though the general solution was for the Orthodox to relax their standards for the day in the interest of peace and community, and it was not an active controversy as much as a source of anxiety to those of stricter observance. But I could not help feeling that this was more a compromise than a meaningful resolution.

One result of our occasional attendance at Beit HaDerekh was that Dad and I began talking about what worship music should be like. The pop-like music that was typically sung was often conducive neither to worship nor to congregational singing. Our thought at this time was not particularly developed, but we both felt the current practice was unworkable. At a minimum, music must be reasonably easy for a congregation with minimal familiarity with the song to sing, it should not be smattered with unnecessary Hebraisms that served only as a kind of showing off, and it needed to be genuinely directed toward praise or petition.

It was Ben who first introduced me to the scholarship of the New Perspective on Paul as an answer to the difficulties we had in interpreting his theology in terms of Hebrew Roots theology. We had a twofold problem stemming from our relationship to the Torah. First, what was the Galatian controversy about, if not—as the Protestants said—about the passing away of the Torah? And second, assuming we were right that believers had an obligation to keep the Torah, what did that say about the identity of Gentile believers in relation to Jews? We were, for the most part, committed to avoiding any kind of supersessionism, or replacement theology, but that made it somewhat difficult to explain what it meant that we were right about the Messiah and genealogical Israel was wrong and that our belief in the Messiah indicated that we belong to "the commonwealth of Israel" (Eph 2:12) and that we were responsible for Torah observance.

We were naturally inspired to look for solutions to these problems in the New Perspective, an academic movement begun in the late 1970s by E. P. Sanders when he published his epoch-making *Paul and Palestinian Judaism*. Much like the slightly earlier third Quest for the Historical Jesus, in which Geza Vermes was a key player, the New Perspective sought to situate Paul in his ancient Jewish context by comparing his writings with other surviving Second Temple Jewish witnesses. It will surprise no one familiar with Sanders' work to know that hardly any of us actually read it, but we nonetheless appealed to him and other New Perspective scholars as authorities for what we were doing.

Our argument on the Galatian controversy and the Council of Jerusalem in Acts 15 was that the question was not about absolute requirements but about "entrance requirements". We reasoned that because the Torah is an entire legal code and lifestyle that takes time to learn, it was impossible for new converts to enter into it all at once. A controversy, therefore, arose over which were the first things they would be required to observe in order to belong to the community, and particularly whether circumcision should be imposed immediately. The conclusion reached at the Jerusalem Council was that circumcision was not required for new converts to enter the community, but we claimed it would be expected of them eventually as they grew in their faith. In this approach, we had some support from Sanders' similar conclusions.[5]

This interpretation created a certain difficulty in understanding our relationship to the Jewish people, though. It was clear in the text of the Torah that these laws were specifically intended for the descendants of Jacob, to distinguish them from all others, the Gentiles, and that we did not claim physical descent from Jacob. While both the Messiah and Paul indicated that the "children of Abraham" were more than only the physical descendants of Abraham, and even Judaism claimed belief in "spiritual children" for Abraham, we found it difficult to accept any of the proffered interpretations. The Jewish one was much too deterministic, claiming that if a person was not born with a "Jewish soul", he was forever destined to be a Gentile and outside the community of Israel, even though righteous Gentiles were laudable. On the other hand, Paul's "grafting on" metaphor in Romans 11 had the unsavory implication that at least some of the Jewish people had been replaced by Gentiles, a possibility that many of us were unwilling to accept.

Our solutions had various names, but they were all related and similar. The "two house" theory was derived from Ezekiel 37 and Zechariah 11, in which Israel and Judah are symbolically represented by staffs. In Zechariah, a staff is broken, representing the breaking of the covenant of God with the people. In Ezekiel, the two staffs, one for Israel and one for Judah, are bound together, representing

[5] E. P. Sanders, *Paul, the Law, and the Jewish People* (Minneapolis: Fortress Press, 1983), 17–45.

the final reunification of the kingdom of Israel. The "two house" view argued that the breaking of the staff represented the end of God's covenant with the northern tribes, which made way for the inclusion of the Gentiles without affecting the covenant with the southern tribes of Judah, Benjamin, and Levi.

Related to this, but technically distinct, was the "one new man" position, which essentially accepted the "two house" view as a premise but argued from Ephesians and Ezekiel 37 that it could not be left there. The two staffs had to be bound into one, as Ezekiel describes, and made into "one new man", according to Ephesians 2. No one was left out, but there was also no separation between the two. The New Israel was made up of both the Jews and the believing Gentiles without separation.

There remained some obvious objections to these approaches. The "two house" theory seemed to re-erect the "dividing wall" that Paul was so clear had been torn down (Eph 2:14, RSV-2CE). In Christ, there is no more Jew or Greek, as he writes in Galatians 3:28. The "one new man" position had the advantage of a better reading of Paul, but it still stumbled over the fact that Ephesians 2 explicitly referred to one of the parties as uncircumcised "in the flesh" (2:11). This had to be taken as entirely metaphorical, despite the obviously concrete nature of the statement, in order to reconcile it with our expectation that Gentile converts would eventually conform entirely to the same Torah as Jewish believers. Saint Paul's advice for everyone to remain as they were when they converted, whether circumcised or not, in 1 Corinthians 7 was difficult to square with this position as well. Saint Paul was simultaneously affirming each person in his position regarding the Torah and insisting that there was no separation or distinction between the two, which seemed to imply some relaxation of laws that would inherently cause separation—in the case of Galatians, specifically relating to food laws and table fellowship.

Radical parties took devastating steps to resolve the problem. One teacher began by rejecting the Epistle to the Hebrews—which made the change to the law explicit (Heb 7:12)—citing its lack of attribution to an apostolic author. But he was moderate compared with the other party, the true Ebionites. The historians told us of either a "twofold party of the Nazarenes" or of two sects: the Nazarenes and the Ebionites. The Nazarenes had an orthodox Christology, while the Ebionites had an exceedingly low Christology, viewing the Messiah as merely a man and not born in special circumstances.[6] Ironically, the largest group that rejected the divinity of Christ called themselves "Nazarenes", not Ebionites, but that name was claimed by more Christologically orthodox groups as well.

Although these ideas did not gain traction in Midland, it was easy to encounter them online. Adherents of the Ebionite position tended to be highly Orthodox in their practice of the Torah and rejected the divine nature of the Messiah. They rejected the entire New Testament except some version of the Gospel of Matthew, or the Gospel of the Hebrews. In many ways, it was a very appealing solution: it had internal consistency and allowed greater integration with the Jewish community and a definite rule of life that was shared among all of its followers. Their solution to the problem of identity was to refer to the Messiah's movement as merely a form of Judaism, so following Him required full conversion to Orthodox Judaism. But from what Kreeft and Lewis had taught me, it was also clearly not a workable solution. It relied on the hypothetical reconstruction of a lost Gospel, in the face

[6] Pritz, *Nazarene Jewish Christianity*, 30–35.

of our best evidence about what the earliest Christians believed and taught about the risen Messiah. It solved all our problems but created a host of new and worse ones. At the same time, in order to compete with the Ebionites' claim to antiquity, I firmly embraced the title of Nazarene or Netzari Judaism.

None of the proffered solutions was satisfactory to me, so I remained systematically agnostic while holding on to several specific features that any successful theory had to have:

1. It had to include a robust view of the union of Jews and Gentiles in alignment with Saint Paul's tearing down "the dividing wall" and "neither Jew nor Greek" claims.
2. It had to make sense of the claim that some native branches of Israel had been removed to make way for the Gentiles and that this was the result of the gospel.
3. There had to be no second-class citizens, as all are "fellow citizens with the saints, and of the household of God" (Eph 2:19).
4. It had to be not merely theoretical but practical, extending to very concrete matters regarding table fellowship and the sharing of food (see Gal 2:12–14).
5. It had to allow for the prophet Isaiah's claim that the Gentiles would observe the same Sabbath as the Jews and would be required to celebrate the feast of Tabernacles at the Temple (see Is 56:6; Zech 14:16–19).
6. It could not involve hypothetical reconstructions and re-forming the evidence to suit our preconceived theology.

This was a tall order, and nobody seemed to be filling it.

8

This knotty ecclesiological problem tied in with a theme the Houston group was pursuing on other grounds: the Mystical Bride of the Messiah. They strongly emphasized the importance of the community as Bride and taught this mystical theology largely from the Song of Songs. For them, it especially meant the pursuit of sanctity following the holiness laws of Leviticus, symbolized by the adornment of the Bride in Psalm 45. Even as a Baptist I had been vaguely aware that the Church is the Bride of Christ, but it was not emphasized, and I had little notion of more than the bare statement. Learning what it means to be the Bride with regard to receptivity, readiness, purity, and wholeness was eye-opening and at the same time uncomfortable. Ours was a very masculine environment, which I do not consider to be a negative, but it was important and difficult to balance that patriarchal emphasis with this discovery that in our relationship to God we are collectively feminine. It gave the mystery a symmetry and a depth I had not encountered before, and it made me deeply uncomfortable in a good way.

One of the most common refrains of the Hebrew Roots Movement, from Michael Rood to Ted Pierce's popular song "Come Out of Her, O My People", was that the culture—and, according to some, the Christian church—was the Whore of Babylon. Most commonly, at least implicitly, the counterpart to this Babylon was something we were moving toward, an eschatological Israel.

Teachers may have acknowledged theoretically that we already belonged to her, but she was something to do with the prophecies of Revelation about the future, and her presence here and now was not emphasized. So the Houston group's focus on the fact that we were already, if only in part, the heavenly Bride was revolutionary. Our journey was no longer a mere exodus from Babylon into a future that did not seem to be getting any closer as time went on but a real setting out from one city for another, even if she was at this point nascent, a tabernacle rather than a temple. She may have been a bedouin city, but she was a real city.

Tied in with this, at least from my perspective, was the Houston group's distinctive mode of dress. At festivals and on Sabbaths, and occasionally during the week, many of them wore brightly colored tunics with long slits up the sides and their tzitziot attached to the corners. Compared with the rest of us, they truly looked like priests. Thus were we introduced to Beged Ivri and the work of Reuven Prager. Reuven was one of the most fascinating people I have ever met. He was an Orthodox Jew living in Jerusalem and a descendant of the tribe of Levi who took his Levitical duty seriously. He dedicated much of his life to the restoration of Jewish customs from the biblical period, including extensive research into the spices used to make the incense for the Temple, the proper weight of a biblical shekel, and biblical clothing. The latter led him to found his tailoring enterprise, Beged Ivri (Hebrew garment). The tunics he made were something of a concession to modern clothing, an effort to split the difference between the long outer garment worn by ancient Israelites—usually translated "cloak"—and a modern shirt. The most important element for Reuven was that the tzitziot were meant to be worn on the outer garment, not hidden under the clothes.

Reuven made periodic trips to America to sell his wares and promote his work on restoring ancient customs, including the redemption price of the firstborn, called *pidyon haben* (see Ex 13). Unlike many people who made the rounds to raise money, Reuven made no promises, and he offered a great deal in return, both in terms of well-researched education and in wonderful products. I had not seen or spoken with him in years when he went to his reward early in 2023, but Reuven will always be dear to my heart. *Requiem aeternam dona eis Domine.* My family bought several tunics and eventually one of the great biblical cloaks, though we kept them all for special occasions, which somewhat undercut the purpose of the tunic.

This restoration idea, the clothes and the lifestyle they implied, were deeply countercultural. I feel grateful that we did not try to make our belief cool, though we embraced its cooler elements. The Orthodox reggae artist Matisyahu was popular at the time, and I loved listening to his music. I had "King without a Crown" and "Someday" memorized for a long time. But I embraced the countercultural idea. I adopted the plain dress of T-shirts and polos without words or logos with blue jeans for most days and khakis for special occasions, and when I turned sixteen, I had no interest in learning to drive. A number of factors contributed to that decision, but to my mind, it became a symbol of my resistance against modernity, against the culture of "Babylon". I walked the mile and a half to Starbucks when I needed to get out of the house, and I rode my bicycle a couple of miles to see friends, even in the ninety-five-degree West Texas summer heat, and I in my customary black. But mostly I was happy to stay at home and study.

It was this unusual combination of traditional and restorationist Judaism that was practiced in Houston, and on our occasional trips there, I was drawn to it quite strongly. My family celebrated the feast of Tabernacles with this group at least once more while I was in high school. Their leadership worked hard to live and serve like priests, keeping ritual purity laws, with coherent rules for community life. They wanted to be holy, which Mr. O—— repeatedly defined as "following God's loving, teaching instruction". They were imperfect, but they made a sincere effort. For them, the tradition was a kind of historical thread, not wholly reliable but useful for reconstructing the past and venerable, not to be dismissed lightly.

By the age of sixteen, I had been studying Hebrew for two years but had largely stalled, and I had trouble discerning how to proceed. Mom and Dad looked for a tutor and found one in the form of Dr. T——. He was a doctor of Old Testament whose liberal education and theological conservatism combined to make it difficult to find a job either at a seminary or a major university, so instead he taught Spanish at one of the high schools in Odessa. But he moonlighted as a Hebrew tutor, and I was his first pupil.

Dr. T—— introduced me to Weingreen's *Hebrew Grammar*, the one I continue to use when I teach Hebrew to this day. For my homework each week, I was to read a chapter of Weingreen, which I largely understood, and when we met one evening a week in his study, we would read as many verses of Genesis as we could get through in an hour. He would go on long, wonderful excurses that I did not understand about Hebrew syntax and vocabulary, and I would try desperately to follow along, utterly entranced and utterly uncomprehending. It was a wonderful hour in the dim study, piled high with books and papers in disarray, and he would explain his peculiar theories about classical Hebrew pronunciations and how the language that Jesus often used was not Aramaic but Hebrew, based on the phrasing and the syntax of the Greek New Testament. It was an hour that smelled of musty books, of parchment and ink. I felt like a scribe training in an ancient scriptorium, closely watched by a master scribe pouring out wonderful and incomprehensible minutiae of grammar. He was my Dr. Cornelius and I his Prince Caspian.

It always bothered me that no one in the Hebrew Roots or Messianic communities could teach me Hebrew. I had to go to a traditional Christian to learn it. And his detailed knowledge of the New Testament and of the language of the Messiah disturbed me. The members of my community laid claim to special knowledge and often said things like "If the Christians only knew what we know", but there was nothing I knew that Dr. T—— did not. I had no new information to give him, except a few marginalia. He was decidedly more expert in Judaica than I was, and yet he was not in the Hebrew Roots Movement. At the time, I was able to dismiss this incongruity, but it would stick with me and resurface later.

At some point late in my high school years, I began to reject the Trinity as doctrine. I remember a conversation with one of my Christian internet friends, Klaus, in which I told him this, and he asked, "Well, which Person of the Trinity do you reject?"

But I knew my New Testament better than that. "None of them", I said.

"Then do you think they are separate entities, like the Mormons and the Jehovah's Witnesses do?"

"Of course not."

"So, do you reject the personhood of one of them?"

"Not exactly."

"Then what is the problem?" he pressed.

"I just don't think that's how it works. It's too specific. Too tidy. And the language of it is not there in Scripture. I would accept either the Trinity or the Sefirot as an acceptable metaphor for the nature of God, but neither one as literally true of Him."

That is where the conversation ended. It must be remembered that I was becoming desperate at this point for the Hebrew Roots Movement to be accepted by the mainstream of Judaism, and the Trinity was one of the main sticking points between us. I thought if our doctrine of God was vaguer and more mystical—by which I really meant metaphorical and imprecise—it would narrow the gap.

I need to share briefly one final story because, though it did not have an enormous impact on me, it speaks to the incredible strength of character that my sister possesses, which will inform events to come. When Melody graduated from high school, she wanted to pursue midwifery as a career, so she went to an out-of-state training program operated by conservative charismatics. Shortly after she got there, the feast of Trumpets arrived, and although she thought she had an understanding with the school, they refused to allow her to take the day off. Melody was resolute and refused to compromise her convictions by attending classes, so she was summarily kicked out of the program and sent home. Though she was devastated, she came home and began apprenticing with local midwives while attending classes at the local junior college. Even though my convictions have since changed, I have always been incredibly proud of her conviction.

Part III

Jerusalem (2008–2012)

9

It almost goes without saying that I did not trust the establishment—academic or theological—and that meant that, despite my academic bent, I was convinced throughout high school that I did not want to study the Bible or theology at a university. I was not entirely clear on what else I should do, though I toyed with the idea of studying agronomy. Our community placed a high value on agricultural work because of its significance in the Bible, and most tried to incorporate some kind of gardening or animal husbandry into their lives, to the extent that their situation allowed. But while I found science fascinating as a kind of hobby, I did not particularly excel at it, and it did not preoccupy me the way Hebrew and the Bible did.

So, when I finished high school in 2008 and still had not come to a conclusion, I decided to take a gap year. During the summer, I worked for a builder, mostly cleaning up after the subcontractors. It was solitary work, and I loved it. My boss would drop me off at a site after everyone else had finished, debris everywhere, and my job was to load the garbage onto a trailer to be hauled off to the dump. I had no complaints.

All summer I saved up money, and in August, my grand adventure began. It started as a family trip to Israel, but because I had no real plans for the fall, my parents suggested that I stay behind for the full three months that I was allowed on a tourist visa and volunteer through World Wide Opportunities on Organic Farms (WWOOF). I leapt at the idea. I could spend three months in the Holy Land learning about agriculture, improving my Hebrew, making connections, and becoming deeply invested in this place I was meant to love. It was ideal!

The first hiccup happened at the airport in New York, where, due to flight delays, we missed our connection to Israel. The airline tried to reschedule us, but they could not get four seats on any one flight. The best they could offer was three seats on one direct flight to Tel Aviv and another that would arrive an hour later, with a connection through Paris. This was supposed to be my big adventure, so I immediately volunteered for the Paris flight. On my end, things went off without a hitch, but my parents and sister sat on a runway in Newark for hours on end. When I arrived in Tel Aviv, instead of being met by my parents, I was met by Mrs. O——. Jet-lagged and bewildered, I listened as she explained that the rest of my family would not be arriving for several hours but that her family happened to be in Israel at the time and that she would take me to the hotel on the outskirts of Jerusalem where we had our reservations. I rode there in a daze, checked into the hotel, passed out on the couch, and did not wake up until the rest of my family arrived six hours later.

This trip was different from our previous trip. We stayed nearer the heartland, especially in Judea near Beth Shemesh and in Jerusalem. The most memorable part of the trip was the day we rode in an armored bus through the West Bank to visit one of our contacts, the former mayor, in Shiloh. The city of Shiloh was the site of the Tabernacle from the time the Israelites entered Canaan under Joshua until King David established his capital at Jerusalem and brought the Tabernacle there. In recent times, it has become a symbol of the contention over the West Bank, as traditionalist Israelis point to it as a site of ancient heritage and assert their right to live there, while Palestinians decry the settlement as illegally seized from them without warrant. The contention has led to bloodshed; our guide's son was nearly killed in an attack when he was five or six years old. As a result, Shiloh has developed an extensive program for helping children recover from post-traumatic stress disorder as well as physical injuries. I am not going to enter into Israeli-Palestinian issues here because I cannot do them justice in the middle of this narrative. At the time, I had a very flattened, two-dimensional view on the issue, but now, fifteen years later, my understanding of the situation is entirely too complex to reduce to slogans and brief summaries.

Shiloh was a fascinating experience. The Jews there have built their synagogue in the shape of the Tabernacle as a reminder of their history, but other than that, it is a modern Israeli town, and the people there are not particularly interested in the restoration of ancient customs, as many of our contacts in Jerusalem were. It sits atop a midsize hill, a small settlement surrounded by scrubland, itself green and covered with trees. A modern town with a modern synagogue in the biblical heartland left me with an odd feeling of disjuncture.

Back in Jerusalem we visited the museum of the Temple Institute with some Hebrew Roots acquaintances. The Temple Institute is an organization dedicated to restoring the customs and instruments of the priesthood in preparation for the Temple's rebuilding. These customs were of deep interest to the Hebrew Roots Movement, which looked for the rebuilding of the Temple as a sign of the end times, though we were divided over whether reestablishing the sacrificial cultus of Temple worship was actually a good thing. Though many of us viewed the sacrifice of Yeshua as superseding or even nullifying the animal sacrifices of the Temple, it was hard, when our entire life was focused on the restoration of biblical law and custom, not to be enthusiastically in favor of this project.

The entrance was in a narrow alleyway among the overshadowing limestone row houses of the Old City. (A recent Google search suggests it may have moved to a more visible location, though it is also possible that my confusion was due simply to unfamiliarity with Jerusalem's streets.) We could not have found it without guides, and it made me feel very much like being initiated into the heart of Jerusalem, into the depth of her antiquity. It may have been a museum, but it was the most tucked away of museums, and the great mass of tourists never wandered this far. The museum was fascinating, displaying a combination of ancient discoveries and new restorations: elaborately embroidered garments, ancient fragments of artifacts, raw materials for making incense and cloaks, a beautiful golden censer, and a host of other implements. I associate it with the scents of both incense and must, though I believe at the time I actually smelled neither.

I had my first opportunity to serve as an interpreter there. The group of Hebrew Roots believers who came after us had difficulty communicating with the two young Israeli women operating the admission table. The Americans could not understand Hebrew, and the Israelis had very limited English. It did not help my growing ego that I was able to step in and carry out the extremely basic communication of telling the tourists how much a ticket cost. I knew my numbers and how to ask "How much is admission?", which is all that was really required, but I would be remiss to say that it did not go to my head a little. Especially because the other group was more Orthodox than we were.

We prayed at the Wailing Wall; toured Yad Vashem, the vast Holocaust museum; and, of course, went to the Shrine of the Book, where many of the Dead Sea Scrolls are housed and a few are displayed. We hired a guide for the day, and he took us through the archaeological dig at the City of David and showed us the palace that dates to the time of the ancient kingdom of Judah, then up to the Temple Mount, and across to the base of the Mount of Olives. We visited the remnants of Hezekiah's Wall and the famed Old City bookstore Shoreshim, which means "roots". It all had the intoxicating scent of desert winds blowing from antiquity.

We spent other days in the New City, several times visiting the Jerusalem Shuk, the large open-air market, full of stalls of every kind, but especially of food. There were fruits and vegetables, meat and fish, spices and grains in piles and boxes and sacks. I expected everything to be haggled over and prices debated, but most prices were more or less fixed, with only a little haggling here and there, at least for those who were not fluent in Hebrew or Arabic. More importantly, I decided that my favorite falafel stand in the city was the one just across the street, the ironically named Jerusalem Steakhouse. I do not think I could have told you the difference between their falafel and anyone else's, but I was determined to have a favorite, to be the kind of person who had a favorite place in Jerusalem, to feel like a real initiate of the place and the community.

I spent one day taking a train across the Shephela, a region of rolling land between the central hill country and the coastal plain, to Tel Aviv to meet one of my internet friends, Jason. He was a convert from Christianity to Conservative Judaism and one of my most frequent conversation partners. He was astonished to find out I was only eighteen, having assumed I was a grown adult the entire time we had been dialoguing. It was the first time I realized that many of the people I communicated with on the internet were under the impression that I was older. This gave me a more charitable view of some people I thought had been unfairly harsh in response to my questions, not realizing my age and lack of understanding.

After several days in Jerusalem, we moved to stay at a guesthouse in a backyard on a tiny *moshav*, or settlement, called Tzafririm, about an hour from Beth Shemesh. It was a little town that just covered the top of a small hill in the lower Judean hill country, a stone's throw from the Emeq HaElah, the Valley of Elah, where David slew Goliath. Scrubby terebinths dotted the hillsides of long brown grass, but the moshav itself was lushly covered in date palms and green grass and shrubs. It sprawled with a wonderful, homey disorganization, a kind of country ramshackleness familiar to rural and small-town Americans but with a distinct Middle Eastern character resulting from the fact that most of the population were from Jewish communities in the Middle East and North Africa, rather than from Europe and America. I once stumbled upon a hedgehog crossing the road and stood watching for a long while as it trundled through the undergrowth. Our hosts were generous and welcoming and hospitable to a degree familiar in the Mediterranean and the Near East but utterly unknown to most of us in the West.

From Tzafririm, we ranged to Emeq HaElah, Beth Shemesh, Beer Sheba, and the famed kibbutz Netiv Ha-Lamed-He. The guesthouse was small, but it was our own little house for a week or ten days, and it briefly felt like living in the Holy Land. As my family's return flight approached, we went down to visit the farm where I had agreed to volunteer through WWOOF. It was a flat, dusty place on the coastal plain near Gaza and was run by a dedicated, hardworking woman who showed us the quarters for volunteers—a semipermanent tent adjacent to an outhouse. It was not a great prospect for three months. As it turns out, we had miscommunicated. She thought I was coming for three weeks—a long time for tent living but doable—not the three months I intended to stay.

I sometimes wonder whether I should have endured it. It could have been done, and I was young enough to do it, but at the time, we all decided it made more sense for me to find a different occupation for the rest of my time. We returned to Tzafririm at something of a loss. We spoke with our hosts that evening, and they came up with a suggestion. Just the other side of the moshav was a family, brothers Assi and Yossi, with their parents and Assi's wife and daughter, on a sprawling lot with several buildings. They had a caravan—what we would call a mobile home—that they were renovating with the goal of renting it out. At the time, it was not technically livable, but it would do for me, as I was young and in good health.

Assi was a building contractor, and I had a summer's worth of building experience under my belt. I could help him on building projects at home and abroad, and he would give me room and board. I spent the rest of the summer and early autumn in a mobile home with no electricity or running water, the ceiling coated in an astonishingly thick yellow layer of tobacco residue. I laid tile in the living room, cutting pieces using an old hand cutter, scrubbed the tobacco off the ceiling, and painted the walls. I helped Assi lay the rebar for a concrete pad at a national park and helped his father strip olives off the trees on their property. I was not a confident or self-motivated worker, and I think Assi became frustrated with me halfway through my time there, for which I blame myself.

It was deeply informative. Assi was working on a master's degree in archaeology, struggling with his English requirement. I told him I wanted to keep the Torah without the traditions, and he laughed and pointed out with multiple examples that it was impossible. His father plied me with booze made from figs off their own fig trees and cooked omelets with their own eggs, tomatoes, and onions. His wife was a marvelous woman of Moroccan heritage who mothered me as if I were her own.

I spent every Sabbath in the tiny, un-air-conditioned synagogue just off-center of the community. There I fell in love with the Yemenite Hebrew dialect of the rabbi and began to try to learn it. I would sit next to Yossi and try, with gradually increasing success, to keep up with the frenetic pace of Jewish prayer. It was a trial by fire in which I learned to pray the prayer book, the Siddur, and the Jewish way of rocking back and forth during prayer, called shuckling. I also came to love the traditional Jewish liturgy, with its singsong recitations, its chants and melodies, the rhythm of life in a community that did not think of itself as Orthodox or Conservative or Reform but simply as Jewish, with all their various degrees of commitment to observance. I did not see a non-Israeli for two months.

At night and on Sabbaths, I would sit in my stifling room with the small selection of books I had been able to take with me and would study. I set out to go through the entire Psalter and record its headings and themes and try to tie each one to the day, the season, and the hour of prayer for which it was intended. I made charts of titles and themes, trying to find a pattern and despairing. There was no question in my mind that the psalms were intended to form the basis of the liturgy, so each one must have an intended position in it. I loved the synagogue service, but I was disappointed by its limited use of the psalms, the obvious source for Hebrew prayer. I wanted to create a liturgy that would have a place for every psalm—indeed, be structured around the psalms. In that regard, all the liturgies I knew were something of a disappointment, but my own attempt to organize the Psalter was not very fruitful either. I could invent loose connections based on various associations, but it was clear there was nothing particularly objective about this work, and in many cases, I struggled to come up with an appropriate use for a given psalm. The project was overwhelming and seemed hopeless, and I gave it up before the end of the summer.

While I was there, my parents ordered a biblical cloak for me from Reuven, and Assi and I went to Jerusalem to pick it up from his apartment. Reuven's apartment was the best museum in Jerusalem. He had ancient coins and weights from the Second Temple period and the Bar Kokhba Revolt. He had spices and incense from around the world, rare books, all the resources for making biblical garments, and a host of other things I cannot remember or describe: artifacts, volumes of Jewish history and tradition, and materials such as would be found at a bazaar of ancient Judea. Assi and I were kids in a candy shop. As we were leaving, Assi said, "Guys like that should be put in a museum." He meant it as a compliment.

I spent one Sabbath with a Messianic writer and teacher and his family in East Jerusalem. It was a welcome relief from my underground life in Tzafririm, but it did not contribute overall to my theological journey. The most exciting part of it was that on the way there, my bus failed to come, so I hitchhiked from Tzafririm to Jerusalem with a young businessman, a thrilling experience for an American who had never hitched a ride before.

This time in Israel remains special to me. Cutting tile (very badly) on a back lot was a different experience of Israel than my peers were given—and very different from touring. I got the dirt of the place under my nails, and it was a holy experience in a completely different way than I expected, one that, at the time, I did not understand to be particularly holy. I had no mystical sense of transcendence. I had no sudden emotions or revelations, and I was not particularly righteous. And while Assi's family was more welcoming than I could possibly have anticipated—taking me on a long trip across Judea to celebrate the feast of Rosh Hashana at the home of relatives and loading me on a bus to pray at the Wailing Wall with a group of Orthodox young men before Yom Kippur—I never really integrated into the community. My Hebrew was too poor, and I was too shy, too new, and too ignorant. But at the same time, the cycle of the days and the weeks, the continuous prayer at the synagogue, the work, the love, and the discomfort left a permanent impression on me that I find almost completely inexpressible. I didn't leave radically changed, but perhaps my longing to change deepened and was indelibly connected to my home-longing, because in Tzafririm I very much felt that I had my nose pressed up against the windowpane but could not get inside.

10

My return flight coincided with the end of the feast of Tabernacles, so, as the time approached, Dad decided to come and meet me. We would spend the feast in Jerusalem, and though we could not return on the same flight, we would return close together. Mr. T—— and his oldest son came along, as well as another friend and his oldest son. Because Jerusalem fills up at major festivals, we stayed in classrooms of a school that was off for the week, with a number of other Hebrew Roots friends, and they toured around the country a good bit while I stayed in Jerusalem for the feast. We did not have a *sukkah*, a tabernacle, of our own, but every restaurant in Jerusalem had one, and we ate out frequently. I attended prayer at the Great Synagogue of Jerusalem and danced late into the night with the Lubavitcher Hasidim on King George Street. The week was intoxicating, and it was crowned by an email I sent on a whim.

I knew that Nehemia Gordon lived in Jerusalem, so I sent him an email asking if we could meet. After this week, I had to return to my life in Texas and try to discern what my next steps should be, but I still had no idea what I wanted to do. I had turned out to be no good at construction and had not gotten the head start I wanted in agriculture, so I was once more thinking of school, but I wanted to ask Mr. Gordon for his advice. He agreed to meet me in a café in a part of the New City I had never been to before, a little off the tourists' beaten path, though still on a major thoroughfare. He was blunt and iconoclastic, but enthusiastic. He did not really believe me when I said I knew some Hebrew until he saw that I understood and responded to the waiter.

That meeting was something of a wake-up call. I do not recall the exact words, but the message was "What are you doing? Get back to school. You have the potential to be a serious scholar, and you should absolutely pursue it." It was the push I needed. Nehemia then gave me the address and schedule of a Karaite synagogue in Ramla and told me which train to take to get there.

A day or two later, I boarded the train for Ramla and took a cab, on Nehemia's advice, to the obscure location of the synagogue. It was upstairs in an old building, and when I stepped inside, I was briefly taken aback. There were no chairs or benches anywhere, only a thick red carpet covering the whole floor, and congregants were spread around the room with books of prayer, variously standing or kneeling. Kneeling has no part in traditional Jewish worship, in order to avoid the appearance of worshipping anything that might happen to be in front of the person. It is one of those strange departures from the clear biblical precedent that continued to bother me about the tradition. But the Karaites preserved the older custom, for both Judaism and Christianity, though at the time I did not know it. I thought it looked shockingly Islamic. The service was long and bewildering. These were not the prayers I was familiar with, though they consisted of many biblical quotations that I recognized.

The melodies were new, but the style was familiar. The women sat in a balcony apart from the men, and unlike the synagogue in Tzafririm, where women were also set apart in the balcony, these women often participated in leading the prayers. I was dazed through two hours of rising and falling Hebrew chants of a tradition that adhered strictly to the Received Text of the Hebrew Bible and its musical and grammatical notations. The tenth century in Babylon or Egypt leapt to life, and I would not have been surprised to see Jacob al-Kirkisani walk through the door. Afterward, a family adopted me and took me to their home to feed me. I had eaten earlier against the possibility that I would not be able to eat again until I returned to Jerusalem, so I was not particularly hungry and kept politely turning down more servings, until the matriarch of the family simply took my plate away, piled it high, and imperiously said, "Eat!" And so my hands were tied, and I had to make a valiant effort to clean my plate. I failed, but not before I had done sufficient damage to please my hostess.

Nehemia had sent me to that particular synagogue because they were on a different calendar from the other Karaites, and I could attend the end of Sukkot service there days before everyone else finished. It was devastating to me to find that even in the Holy Land, the Karaites could not agree on the calendar. I loved the experience and was sent away with several prayer books that they generously gave me, but I was disappointed as well. Nehemia told me the community in Jerusalem was small and old and not particularly interesting. The oldest Karaite synagogue in Israel was there, but I could not get in when I tried to visit because it was locked. Nehemia said I did not miss much. It was quite different from my experience at the Great Synagogue of Jerusalem and in Tzafririm, and while it was very educational, I could not see the Karaite solution as workable anymore. On a trip to Beth Shemesh, I stopped at a bookstore and bought my first Orthodox Siddur. I did not know if the Jewish tradition of the Oral Torah was an authority, but it seemed to be a necessity.

I spent my last night in Jerusalem with Mr. T—— and his son in the Jerusalem Hostel, and while I thought I should feel sad about leaving, I did not. I felt something of a fog of confusion, a little excitement about going back to school, and a little loss about leaving this stage of my life, but I was not heartbroken about leaving the land of Israel.

Upon my arrival back in Midland, I quickly began preparing for college. It was halfway through the fall semester, so it was too late to apply to universities, but I could start classes at the local junior college in the spring to get general education requirements done before applying for the next year. The rest of the fall was spent applying; testing out of history, English, and college algebra; and racking up community service hours in order to get a scholarship. And in January 2009, I started a full load of courses at Midland College.

At the same time, I was applying to universities for the next year. I was looking primarily at Ancient Near East–oriented programs at Emory, the University of Chicago, the University of Texas, the University of Wisconsin, and the Hebrew University of Jerusalem. On something of a whim, I applied to Dad's alma mater, Baylor University, for their Biblical and Related Languages major. Baylor was in the process of phasing out this program and required all students who wanted to be in it to have a double major. The university recommended that students major in either Religion, an idea I fundamentally rejected, or Linguistics. I did not have a full understanding of what Linguistics was, but my heart leapt at the idea. I loved language, and I discovered a desire I did not know I had: to study the theory of language in greater depth.

Nonetheless, I did not prefer the Baylor program. I did not want to study the Bible as Christian theology because I did not trust Christian theology, and I thought an Ancient Near East program would be more reliable and informative. So, although I applied, I was more interested in the Hebrew-language program at Wisconsin and the Bible program at Hebrew University.

The semester that I spent at Midland College was a fun time, when I made great friends and adjusted to taking college courses. I even had one history class with one of my oldest Hebrew Roots friends, the eldest of the B—— children. But this is a theological biography, and I did not progress very much theologically at the time. I cannot do the wonderful people I met at that time any justice in the context of a theological biography, but I owe them an enormous debt. I was emotionally distraught at the time, feeling more alienated than ever, and the three or four close friends I made that year, with whom I got coffee and watched movies and stayed up late into the night talking about our favorite books and music, were a salve to my coming-of-age angst.

I must mention, though, that I owe to one of these friends, Mackenzie, the discovery that there was more to Tolkien's legendarium than *The Lord of the Rings*. During a movie night at her house, I spotted on a bookshelf *The Children of Hurin*, which was a complete revelation, and she was shocked that I did not already know of it. She gave me the titles of other books that took place in Middle-earth, and I sought out the library's lone, musty copies of *The Silmarillion* and *The Adventures of Tom Bombadil* in the forgotten back of an out-of-the-way branch. They made the otherwise aesthetically barren year back in Midland bearable, and I spent many hours of my summer in the neglected nondenominational chapel at Midland College poring over the maps and lore of *The Silmarillion*, drinking it in like sunlight.

My prayer routine became more developed, but no more consistent. I was torn between the Karaite prayer books, the Orthodox one, and the Messianic one. I loved that the Messianic prayer book incorporated the Lord's Prayer and New Testament canticles alongside traditional Jewish prayers, but it was even poorer in psalms than the other two. I loved the tradition of the Orthodox prayer book, but I was still on the fence about the authority of the tradition and could not bring myself to stick to it every day. I loved the biblicism of the Karaite prayer books, but I needed more instruction in order to make use of them and had grown disillusioned by the Karaites' inability to even agree among themselves. Without a doubt, though, I was done making my own traditions out of whole cloth.

I was undecided about all of this, but I had finally begun to study Jewish tradition in earnest. I acquired a Torah with commentary from the Conservative movement—a gift from a dear friend at Beit HaDerekh named Christo (who has since converted to Judaism)—and a modern Jewish classic *The Concise Book of Mitzvoth*, an introductory guide to Jewish practice in the modern era. I also devoured traditional Jewish material online.

My sister, on the other hand, was having a rapid change of heart about the entire Hebrew Roots project. I did not have detailed discussions with her at this time, but she was quickly becoming convinced that we had been wrong to leave the Evangelical movement in the first place. She was attending a Bible study directed by the campus ministry of a local Church of Christ church and soon began dating one of her friends from that community. It was disconcerting to the family, and we did not take it very well. There was no question of cutting anyone off or of giving an ultimatum—we did not shun—but we made our displeasure very clear. As I mentioned before, though, Melody is a woman of strong convictions and not easily dissuaded, and she began withdrawing herself from the Hebrew Roots Movement.

At the same time, she had decided, for a variety of practical reasons, to delay pursuing midwifery and to apply to universities, with the result that she and I were both accepted to Baylor in the same week. We were offered robust scholarships, and as a result, though I was loath to be perceived as following my big sister, we both accepted. She was pursuing a degree in International Studies, and I was double-majoring in Biblical Languages and Linguistics.

As we prepared to move to Waco over the summer, I began for the first time to study Jewish mysticism seriously. In contemporary Judaism, there is a large ultra-orthodox movement, considered rather fringe, called the Chabad-Lubavitch Hasidim. Many, though not all, of their adherents believe that the seventh and last leader of the movement, Rabbi Menachem Mendel Schneerson, who died in 1994, was the Messiah and that he did not actually die but is merely in occlusion, from which he will soon emerge and inaugurate the Messianic kingdom. This movement had obvious attractions to Messianics, and it also has a strong Web presence. So, through their internet resources, especially Schneerson's own book of mysticism, *The Tanya*, I began to explore Kabbalah.

Kabbalah was helpful to me in formulating ideas about the nature of God and creation, but it never became central to my interests or theology. This was due, in large part, to the fact that I was much more interested in liturgics and in law, or *halakha* (literally, "walking"), than in systematic or mystical theology. One of the things I learned from Ben, my friend from Beit HaDerekh, was that there is a kind of tripartite division in God, or, more accurately, in His "emanations", in this mystical Jewish tradition, just as there is in Christianity. In kabbalistic teaching, there is an idea that while God Himself is *Ein Sof* ("without boundary") a radical and unmeasurable unity, creatures are able to encounter and interact with Him through His emanations, called Sefirot, of which there are ten. The Sefirot exist in a complex hierarchical structure illustrated in three columns, with three Sefirot each in the left and right columns and the remaining four in the middle. Ben's idea was that this was equivalent to the Christian Trinity and could explain the relationship between the New Testament's Father, Son, and Holy Spirit. I found this idea interesting, but I hesitated to commit to a structure that seemed to be more an illustration than an actual doctrine.

The preceding December I had, for the first time, read through the entirety of the Mishnah, Judaism's oldest collection of legal traditions outside the Bible itself, and this had much more firmly grabbed my attention. This text is a compendium of legal knowledge and tradition, compiled mostly in the third century A.D. in an effort to preserve Jewish traditions following the destruction of the Temple and the dispersion of the community.

But the Mishnah, on its own and without any instruction, is difficult to interpret. I was soon blessed to discover the guidance I needed in the form of Jacob Neusner's introductory textbook, *Making God's Word Work*. Neusner points out that the purpose of the Mishnah was to transform the difficult and unorganized laws of the Torah into a system, especially for preserving holiness, in this newly displaced community.[1] It was the Mishnah that made the Torah work. And I was desperate for a way to make the Torah work. I still thought of the tradition as secondary and necessarily subservient to the text of the Torah, susceptible to criticism if I deemed that it disagreed with the text. After all, this seemed to be the position that Yeshua took in Matthew 23, where He criticized the Pharisees for subverting the Torah by their traditions but then turned around and told the people they should observe

[1] Jacob Neusner, *Making God's Word Work: A Guide to the Mishnah* (New York: Continuum, 2004), 11–17.

the tradition, not found in Scripture, of tithing mint, anise, and cumin. The problem was not the tradition itself but when it was opposed to the written Torah.

This compromise was a more elegant way of squaring the circle of the Messiah's hard sayings regarding the "tradition of the elders" and the seat of Moses (Mt 15:2; 23:2) than any of the Karaite-oriented Hebrew Roots solutions. The tradition had authority, but it was secondary and interpretive, not primary, as it was treated in Judaism and Christianity. The necessity of this tradition for unity was abundantly clear to our family as we saw more and more how the community, even where cooler heads prevailed and formal unity was maintained, fragmented over the very practical issues of feast days and ritual purity. It seemed to me, therefore, that the tradition had to take priority over individual preference at times and yet still be subject to criticism from the text of Scripture.

My schedule of prayer continued to grow in firmness over the summer. Judaism has three daily times of prayer: Shacharit in the morning, Mincha at around 3:00 P.M., and Ma'ariv in the evening. The morning and evening prayers are based on the times decreed for the recitation of the Shema, the great prayer of Deuteronomy 6: "when thou liest down, and when thou risest up" (v. 7). The Morning and Afternoon Offices are based on the timing of the two major daily sacrifices of the Temple, and the tradition is that they take the place of those sacrifices for the sustenance of the community. Evening Prayer, though not connected to a required daily sacrifice, is associated with voluntary sacrifices made in the Temple. Specifically filling the role of sacrifice is the central prayer of Judaism: the *Amidah* (the standing prayer), also called the *Shemoneh Esrei* (the "eighteen" benedictions). Jewish tradition traces this prayer to the sages from the time of Ezra, called the Men of the Great

Assembly. The Amidah is so central to Jewish prayer that any service is considered incomplete without it. So, while Morning and Evening Prayer have both the Shema and the Amidah, Afternoon Prayer has only the Amidah.[2]

I was still torn about my tradition. I often prayed from the Orthodox Siddur that I had acquired in Israel, but I had reservations about accepting the whole Tradition, and I wanted the inclusion of specifically Messianic prayers. The latter were provided for me in my Messianic Siddur in the form of New Testament hymns and prayers translated into Hebrew, but that was a greatly abbreviated service, though traditional, and included even fewer psalms. The Karaite prayer books were heavier on Scripture, particularly the psalms, but they were in other ways the worst of both worlds, being neither traditional nor Messianic.

At this time, a new Messianic family moved to the area, and they were very Orthodox in their practice and belief. The father of the family was a convert from Orthodox Judaism who would later return to that faith. They introduced us to an organization called First Fruits of Zion, or FFOZ. Unlike many of the other Messianic and Hebrew Roots teachers and organizations with which I was familiar, the members of FFOZ were not only highly Orthodox but also well educated, abreast of contemporary scholarship and deeply informed by Jewish tradition. Even more importantly, they had begun producing liturgical materials.

My first experience with their liturgy was at dinner with them one Sabbath when, instead of a typical Orthodox booklet for the blessings, they produced a little leather-bound volume that contained all the traditional prayers and

[2] Rabbi Nosson Scherman, ed., *Siddur Ahavat Shalom / The Complete ArtScroll Siddur: Pocket Size—Nusach Ashkenaz*, 2nd ed. (New York: Mesorah Publications, 1987), 30, 90, 98, 110, 232, 256.

blessings for the Sabbath table and also the blessings from the *Didache*—the paragon of early Semitic Christian liturgical texts! The introduction referred to these blessings as the original Sabbath table blessings of the Nazarene and Jewish Christian community. I was shocked and invigorated.

At the same time, I was eager for a complete Siddur in this tradition, and I learned that FFOZ had just such a project underway. The only problem was that it is a truly monumental task to create not only a prayer book but a new tradition of prayer. The Siddur is more like the Book of Common Prayer than like most Catholic prayer books in that it contains almost everything an ordinary Jewish person will need for his prayer life. Some editions are more thorough than others, but ideally the Siddur contains the Daily Offices, the Sabbath Offices, the major festival Offices, blessings for ordinary mealtimes, and the special blessings for mealtimes on Sabbaths and festivals. It also contains blessings for various occasions, such as going on a journey, starting work, or recovering from an illness. The most popular versions produced by ArtScroll contain copious instruction in prayer rites and commentary as well as the entire Psalter. So, though FFOZ began the project in 2006 or 2007 and continues to produce new prayer resources occasionally, as of April 2024 the project has remained incomplete. I point that out not as a critique but merely as an indicator of the monumental nature of the task.

I was most excited about the liturgical work this organization was producing, but there was another important aspect of their work, which sought to fill a gap we had all long been feeling. FFOZ did great work in exploring the origins and prehistory of Messianic Judaism and published many of the writings of early Jewish converts in the eighteenth and nineteenth centuries. Many of these writers were prominent rabbis, or rabbis from prominent families, who converted because they discovered Yeshua as the Jewish Messiah. FFOZ meticulously recovered these long out-of-print texts and published them in its Messianic Luminaries series. The most prominent of these writers were Rabbi Isaac Lichtenstein, the chief rabbi of northern Hungary for much of the nineteenth century who retained his position after coming to believe in Yeshua, and Father Paul Philip Levertoff, the heir to a Hasidic dynasty of rabbis who became an Anglican priest.

Because the Hebrew Roots Movement and Messianic Judaism were revitalized and, to a certain extent, became what they are today as part of the Jesus movement in the 1970s under a great wave of Restorationist fervor, we had not had a great sense of our history. We vaguely appealed to the "first generation" and the apostolic Church, but there was little more than a hand-waving attempt to fill the gap in between. This gap had bothered me ever since I wrote my high school research paper on the history of the sect of the Nazarenes. If this was the true Church, why did the trail go cold in the fifth century? Now that I was invested in finding an interpretive tradition that could provide practical unity to our divided communities, I was bothered even more. The gap in our history seemed to eliminate any possibility of having such a tradition. This effort to connect us to history, even if it was only a bare two hundred years, seemed like the first step in the right direction. If it was possible to read the works of nineteenth-century Messianic rabbis, maybe it was possible to do more, to go further, and to connect with an authentic, maintained interpretive tradition. But twelve hundred years is a long gap. For the time being, because of my middling view of the tradition, the balance could hold.

11

In the fall of 2009, my sister and I moved to Waco and began classes at Baylor University. Because we were transfer students, we were in the same cadre of students for orientation, but beyond that, we rarely saw each other. Also in our group were two students from the Dallas area, Zaynab and Hina, who were cousins and the first Muslims I had met, and I quickly latched on to the prospect of making friends from another Near Eastern tradition. In some ways, I felt more affinity with my Muslim friends than with the Evangelicals around us. We had dietary laws and set hours of prayer, a sacred tongue and ritual purity and an emphasis on divine unity, none of which were present among the Baptists, charismatics, and others at a Baptist school like Baylor. More importantly, we had an emphasis on antiquity and tradition.

In my first semester at Baylor, I took, among other things, Greek, Hebrew, and the required Bible survey course, Christian Scriptures. This was the beginning of a crisis for me. I resisted the mounting evidence against a fundamentalist view of Scripture as long as I could, but my mother had trained me to take evidence very seriously, and I could not simply ignore or dismiss it. Although the Bible survey course was too rapid to go into detail about many of these issues, our professor was a Pentateuch scholar of the German school, and he spent some time detailing the "four-source theory", or documentary hypothesis.

This hypothesis argues that there are four basic sources for the books of Moses (J, E, D, and P) and that they can be distinguished from one another and read as coherent narratives once they are disentangled. These sources, it is argued, are later than Moses, though given dates vary and are somewhat debatable.[1] Most of the evidence of their differences could be disputed, as far as I was concerned, but the fact that they made coherent narratives once they were separated was evidence of a different order from the rest and was not so easily dismissed.

I had been too well trained in reason to make the mistake that many classmates did, of confusing Mosaic authorship with divine authorship. I remember a phone call with Mom in which I assured her that even if the modern scholars were right about Moses, that didn't mean that God was not involved in writing the Torah. I was still confident that however we got the text of the Bible, it was directed by the will of God. But I was distressed about how this might work, how we could have certainty, and what that implied about interpretation of the Bible. If these texts had undergone reworking and reinterpretation in the process of making the Bible, how were we supposed to know what they meant? The meaning of a story in the J source was in some way altered by its being incorporated into the text of Genesis, but how? And did the original meaning still apply in some way? My Christian Scriptures course did not provide any kind of resolution to these and other problems, and I very nearly despaired of understanding the Bible because this made it clear that the views of the traditional Jewish interpreters,

[1] For an accessible overview of the current situation in Pentateuch, see John S. Bergsma and Jeffrey L. Morrow, *Murmuring against Moses: The Contentious History and Contested Future of Pentateuchal Studies* (Steubenville, Ohio: Emmaus Academic, 2023).

who all took Mosaic authorship quite literally, were fundamentally flawed.

This was the unraveling of a great deal of my worldview at the source. The Bible was our authority because it had been handed down in an unbroken chain of succession from Moses, Isaiah, Paul, James, and the others. It had the imprint of the inspired prophets and apostles. The chain of tradition from Joshua through the Men of the Great Assembly to the rabbis was at the core of their interpretive authority, according to the Mishnah.[2] God had guaranteed it by His authority, and, as a result, it was the only reliable authority, so what did it mean that it might not be quite as reliable as I had thought? What if we had been reading it all wrong?

As a result of these concerns, I became extremely interested in early biblical interpretation, especially inner-biblical exegesis, that is, how biblical texts interpret other biblical texts. I spent hours poring over the passages of Ezra and Nehemiah that applied the laws of the Torah to their own practice, but I could not discern a coherent system. The interpretation and application seemed to be very loose and intuitive, rather than rigorous and systematic. I did not go looking for secondary sources covering the topic, but I cannot be sure why. It may be that I did not trust them, or that I was afraid of what I would find, or that I felt too overwhelmed with my questions on top of my schoolwork, or some combination of the three.

I very reluctantly accompanied one of my new friends from Hebrew class, Matt, to a talk by a visiting lecturer that would change my life. A professor from Israel had come to

[2] "Pirkei Avos", chap. 1; Rabbi Nosson Scherman, ed., *Siddur Ahavat Shalom/The Complete ArtScroll Siddur: Pocket Size—Nusach Ashkenaz*, 2nd ed. (New York: Mesorah Publications, 1987), 545.

promote his recently published book, *How to Read the Bible: A Guide to Scripture, Then and Now*. The man was Professor James Kugel, and his work has loomed large over all the research and writing I have done in the thirteen years that have followed. Kugel was addressing exactly the dilemma I faced: What do these modern discoveries mean for the faithful? I ran out and bought a copy of the book as soon as I could, and though it sits on my desk in front of me, I do not need to open it to quote his conclusion: "The texts that make up the Bible were originally composed under whatever circumstances they were composed. What made them the Bible, however, was their definitive reinterpretation" by the people who first called them the Bible.[3]

Kugel exhaustively compared the conclusions of modern scholars with the traditions of both Jewish and Christian interpreters in the early centuries through the length of the Hebrew Bible. His conclusion was that the inspiration or authorization that made the Bible the Bible was not invested in the process of compilation as much as in the process of canonization and interpretation that happened at the turn of the eras. My world would never be the same because it immediately became clear that the tradition was not only not less authoritative than the text of the Bible but that the tradition had *made* the Bible—that they were bound up in each other and inseparable. It might appear that this made the tradition more authoritative, but the reality was, rather, that they could hardly be distinguished. They moved in and out of each other in a kind of perfect dance.

This approach, of course, created a new problem. What was Yeshua talking about in Matthew 23 when He criticized

[3]James Kugel, *How to Read the Bible: A Guide to Scripture, Then and Now* (New York: Free Press, 2007), 681–82.

the Pharisees for subverting the Torah by their traditions? Why did He critique the traditions of the elders if they were an inherent part of reading the Torah? The somewhat uneasy solution was that this was not a critique of the Tradition, properly so called, but of abuses of it. Differences in schools of interpretation were known to us from ancient times, and the generation before the Messiah famously produced two opposing authorities: the rabbis Hillel and Shammai, who frequently disagreed over the application of the Tradition. It seemed to me that Yeshua was talking about the use of these differences to one's own advantage, not the tradition itself. True tradition had to be in harmony with Scripture, but because it was a discursive tradition, it could be abused in order to circumvent the clear mandate of Scripture.

At about the same time, I began to learn just how many more ancient Greek New Testament manuscripts exist than there are of the Aramaic, which began to erode my confidence in the Peshitta. While Aramaic originalists argued that there were no early copies of the Syriac Aramaic New Testament because the Eastern custom was to burn worn-out manuscripts, the fact that not a single fragment of an actual Aramaic New Testament manuscript survived from before the fourth century strained credulity. First Fruits of Zion also did not take the Syriac claims of originality seriously, and while they preferred a nineteenth-century Hebrew translation of the New Testament by the great German Hebraist Franz Delitzsch, this translation was itself based on the Greek, not the Syriac.

In fact, the more I learned about textual criticism, the more compelling the case for a Greek original became. One of the claims of the Syriac originalists was that the Syriac Aramaic version must be the original because it contained fewer variant readings than the Greek manuscript tradition. But variant readings tend to accrue over time through a variety of historical forces, especially copyists' errors. A unified textual tradition is usually a sign of a later, centralized harmonization. It was actually a strike against the Peshitta that it had so few variants.

Once again, this led to a new problem, but one that I largely dismissed. The great thing about the Peshitta was that its quotations of the Old Testament were, with few exceptions, very similar to the traditional Hebrew text. In the case of the Greek New Testament, however, the majority of its quotations of the Old Testament are based on the Greek translation, the Septuagint. For those committed to the Jewish tradition, this posed a serious problem. The tradition is supposed to include the text of the Hebrew Bible, divinely preserved by the same mechanisms that preserved the Oral Torah. Why, then, did the New Testament frequently quote the Greek version, even when it disagreed with the Hebrew?

Ben was fond of referring to these discrepancies as "paraphrases" and leaving it at that. But their overlap with the Septuagint was too consistent for that to be entirely satisfactory as an explanation. It was more complete to say they had followed the Septuagint because *it* was a paraphrase, where it did not contradict the contents of the Hebrew Bible. The only exceptions, in texts such as Psalm 22, were supported by some Hebrew manuscripts as well, either the Dead Sea Scrolls or a minority of copies of the traditional version of the Hebrew Bible, the Masoretic Text. While this solution itself creates problems for the idea of an unimpeachable Hebrew text, I did not pursue the question too far and so found it reasonably satisfactory. It remained an irritant in the back of my mind that I could not entirely dismiss but chose to ignore for the time being.

Heady theological problems aside, I had a more practical problem on the ground in Waco: I could find no Messianic or Hebrew Roots congregation nearby that met regularly. I was utterly resistant to the idea of attending a church, but I was quickly attempting to join the Jewish mainstream. The summer before I left for college, I had finally buckled to the modern world and gotten my driver's license, so the obvious solution for me, because I did not want to "forsake the assembling", in the words of Hebrews 10:25, was to attend the Conservative Jewish synagogue across town as often as I could. When the rabbi there found out who I was, he pulled me aside and made sure I did not have any intention of proselytizing his congregation. I assured him I did not. I justified this decision by telling myself that I needed a community, and because I did not have any other, it did not make sense to alienate myself from the only synagogue where I could pray regularly.

The building was midcentury and nondescript, and so few congregants attended regularly that weekly services were held in the library rather than the main sanctuary. Services were simple and traditional, of a kind of beauty that remains very close to my heart. Chant was led competently and without show or embellishment, and in keeping with Jewish tradition, there was no accompaniment. It was plain, devout, humble, clear, and sublime.

At Baylor, I was able to study with wonderful professors, notably my Hebrew professor, James Nogalski, who distinguished himself not only because he was a great scholar but also because he was caring and, important for new students, approachable. The other major new influence in my intellectual formation was the now-famous coffeehouse adjacent to campus, Common Grounds. It was our salon, the meeting of a few great minds and a great many mediocre ones, which I had been craving and which Midland simply did not provide. At Common Grounds, I quickly fell in, though I do not remember how, with a number of students from Baylor's accompanying divinity school, Truett Theological Seminary. They indulged me, or were amused by me, or were just happy to spend time with someone who never tired of talking about theology, and I loved to tag along with people who were invested in the subject that consumed me. One of these, Lance, was in the process of transferring from the Baptist church to a church of which I was only vaguely aware: the Anglican church.

For the next three years, when I was not at the library, I lived largely at Common Grounds, where I finally acquired a taste for black coffee, which has sustained me ever since. At the time, Common Grounds had a Mexican High-Grown Chiapas that was eye-opening in more ways than one. At almost any hour of the day and late into the night, someone was there who wanted to discuss ideas, and there was nothing I wanted more than to discuss ideas. Almost any idea would do. I made most of my friends at Baylor simply by horning in on others' conversations at Common Grounds, and in that environment, it was usually considered acceptable. It was a place not only for meeting with friends but also for meeting strangers, something I have rarely encountered elsewhere. It was the closest thing I could imagine to paradise.

As I was becoming more and more serious about studying Jewish tradition, my parents bought me a full set of Jacob Neusner's edition of the Talmud, which I embraced with alacrity. Once again, I was particularly preoccupied by the subject of the liturgy, especially the Daily Offices, and I tried to make myself as fully acquainted with the rules surrounding them as I could. About this time, I also began reading the great medieval rabbi Moses Maimonides' *Guide for the Perplexed*, which gave me my first introduction to Aristotle and Scholasticism.

In the spring of 2010, my understanding of Christianity suffered another blow as the result of a required course. At 8:00 A.M. on Mondays, Wednesdays, and Fridays, I took Christian Heritage, an overview of Christian history, with a well-prepared graduate student who did not anticipate a highly caffeinated early riser like me. I ruthlessly interrogated him about the Great Apostasy and Constantine, to the endless annoyance of my groggy classmates. While I was not satisfied to take his word for it and insisted on checking as many primary documents as I had time to read, it did not help that he was an Anabaptist and, in many respects, not theologically sympathetic to the great Fathers of the fourth and fifth centuries. And yet he did not confirm Messianic theories about pagan infiltration, or the Great Apostasy. He argued that the Church had gradually and without malice accrued errors that needed to be corrected by the Reformation, but he had none of my vitriol and in fact dispelled many of my ideas about the pagan origins of Christian practices.[4] This was the beginning of two or three years of discovering that everything I thought I knew about traditional Christianity was wrong.

I followed up on claims that Christmas was likely not based on Saturnalia, but it looked as if the best evidence was against me. Easter also appeared to be merely a different calculation for Passover, and I learned that the rest of the Christian world called it *Pasch* or *Pascha*, and "Easter" seemed to be from "East", not from an unattested

[4] See Peter G. Cobb, "The History of the Christian Year", in *The Study of the Liturgy*, ed. Cheslyn Jones, Geoffrey Wainwright, and Edward Yarnolds, S.J. (New York: Oxford University Press, 1978), 403–18.

goddess, Eostre. In fact, as hard as I looked, I could find vanishingly little evidence for a great many "pagan origins" claims. There were hints here and there—Christmas trees seemed solidly pagan, for example[5]—but they were also peripheral to Christian traditions and, until the twentieth century, were purely regional. Christmas itself was based on the symbolism of the equinox and some debatable calculations regarding when Jesus was actually born or conceived, but almost certainly not on Saturnalia, whose origins appeared to be slightly *later* than those of Christmas. And so, although I still believed that these Christian practices were wrong, particularly in that they were departures from the biblical practices, they were merely mistaken, not malicious, deformations.

The spring yielded few other developments in my theological outlook, as I simply dug into Jewish tradition to gain a wider acquaintance with it. The Hasidic Chabad-Lubavitch movement continued to play a large role in this process, simply because its resources were easily accessible online. I also acquired a copy of one book from the Messianic Luminaries series, Paul Philip Levertoff's *Love and the Messianic Age*, which reframed the gospel message in terms of the Hasidic movement's mystical theology. It was a moving and compelling book and offered clarity on what I had been trying to work out. Importantly, it made little reference to the Sefirot and other kabbalistic frameworks and was basically orthodox in its outlook.

I believe it was over that winter break of 2009 to 2010 that I stumbled upon a copy of the 1979 Book of Common Prayer (BCP), which had been relegated to a used

[5] I have since learned that I was at least partly wrong even about this tradition, despite its pagan appearance. See Joseph Ratzinger, "The Tree of Life", in *The Blessing of Christmas*, trans. Brian McNeil (San Francisco: Ignatius Press, 2005), 51–62.

bookshop because it was bound upside down. It interested me as a kind of Christian Siddur,[6] but, with no framework for Christian liturgy, I did not really understand it. As I pursued Levertoff's thought and read his Messianic liturgy, *The Meal of the Divine King*, I was at first confused because this did not look like any Jewish liturgy with which I was familiar. Once I began to explore the BCP, this other form of prayer suddenly came into clear relief. Levertoff had taken the framework of the Anglican liturgy, substituted traditional Jewish prayers and blessings for some of the Christian ones, centered the first part of the service, the Liturgy of the Word, on the Torah rather than on the Gospel, and written a new Communion Prayer, heavily dependent on Isaiah. It was less a Messianic Jewish liturgy than a Hebrew Christian one. The form was Christian and the content Judaized, whereas I was used to a Messianic liturgy whose form was Jewish and its contents Christianized.

That baffled me because Levertoff's project did not seem to be the same as mine or as FFOZ's. He was showing a fundamental compatibility between Jewish and traditional Christian theology, but he was not liturgically committed to Jewish tradition, as I was. It was exciting to discover that this very learned Messianic clergyman had written a liturgy, but it was quite disappointing to read it. I was still looking for a liturgy that would be our own, and while I overwhelmingly relied on my Orthodox Siddur now, I still found myself occasionally returning to Rabbi Fisher's *Siddur for Messianic Jews* to answer this longing, but it remained unsatisfactory, ahistorical, and all but completely lacking in psalms.

[6] Years later, I would discover an outstanding book on this premise: Rabbi Chaim Raphael, *A Jewish Book of Common Prayer* (London: Weidenfeld and Nicolson, 1986).

I fear I am giving the impression that I do not, or did not, like Rabbi Fisher's Siddur. On the contrary, I like it very much, and in many ways it was my ideal prayer book. But I was bothered by these gaps in our tradition that it represented. I am still fond of the book and occasionally use it to supplement my prayer routine, which is why it was so devastating that it did not satisfy all that I wanted in a Siddur. It was a symbol of the failure of our whole movement.

My interest in prayer began to focus in many ways on its connections to Temple ritual. In the Jewish tradition, not only does the Amidah, as mentioned previously, take the place of the daily sacrifices, but the rules regarding the daily sacrifices from the Torah, the Mishnah, and the Haggadah are recited at the beginning of Morning Prayer. This is a kind of practice called a *Zecher*, a memorial. It is a practice that both recalls and counts as fulfilling a commandment that can no longer be fulfilled literally.[7] So the recitation of the sacrifices, like the recitation of the story of the Exodus at Passover, relives the event.[8] Jewish tradition treats a Zecher as a kind of divine fiat, that God has declared an equivalence between the two, which He accepts because it is His offering to accept as He chooses.

By the time I returned to Midland for the summer, the community at Beit HaDerekh, where my parents now regularly attended, had become aware of my intensive study of the Siddur. I was invited to give a lecture on the Siddur—its basic contents, use, and meaning—after the service. It was

[7] For a philosophical explanation of ritual as reentering the time of mythic history, or reenacting the myth, see Mercia Eliade, *Myth and Reality*, trans. Willard Trask (New York: Harper and Row, 1963).

[8] The Passover ritual meal, the Seder, includes a prayer called the *Bekhol dor vador*, meaning "in every generation", which states that all Jewish people for all time are to consider themselves as if they were delivered from Egypt with that first generation, based on Exodus 13:8 and Deuteronomy 6:23.

well received, and I was asked for a transcript of the talk so that people could learn better to pray according to the tradition.

That summer I also began my long flirtation with socialism, primarily in reaction to a professor at Midland College. The sociology professor had just retired, and a psychology professor was teaching the sociology course that summer. To keep on track to graduate, I took courses every summer during college, and I ended up in his class. When discussing Marxist conflict theory, the professor summarily dismissed all socialist systems as legal theft. He had seen me ride my bike to campus and insisted that socialism meant that anyone could just take my bike while I was in class, and he refused to allow me to respond. I decided on the spot, as a reaction to his insolence, that I was a socialist. It was a doomed relationship from the beginning.

I never had a desire for a centralized state to control all means of production, nor did I desire the absolute abolition of private property. I was, however, becoming disillusioned with the ideas of laissez-faire capitalism and the self-regulating market. Although I accepted the Jewish tradition that the division of the land and the Jubilee, in which everyone returns to their ancestral inheritance and no one is without an inheritance of real estate, was a unique situation meant for the Holy Land, I could not help thinking that it indicated something about economic ethics. Provision had to be made to ensure that no one became part of a permanent underclass, and it did not appear that the free market was up to the task. But socialism's concerns are beyond this, and Marx's ideas are more radical. It was clear that conflict theory had some explanatory power, but, at the same time, it was clearly not workable as a universal theory of human society to say everything could be summarized as a clash between the classes.

In the fall of 2010, I returned to Baylor and began my study of introductory linguistics. This was an exciting time for me intellectually, and while I enjoyed all aspects of the introductory course, I was most taken with semantics and pragmatics, whose implications for the interpretation of the Bible were immediately obvious. These are the subfields of linguistics that deal with language meaning and meaning in context. I was still trying to work out my own theory of hermeneutics—that is, the interpretation of texts—and how it related to the Tradition. This was a somewhat thorny issue in Judaism, which has no one central authority for interpreting the tradition but rather a system of *semichah*, ordination by the laying on of hands, which transfers authority from rabbi to rabbi. Sources of tradition gradually gain authority over time as they are accepted by the general community of Israel, or of Orthodoxy, and texts and teachers may have different degrees of authority, depending on the depth and breadth of their acceptance.

I was particularly concerned with how Yeshua fit into this structure because He must be considered our ultimate authority, but He was not generally accepted by the community of Israel. Furthermore, the tradition that had been developing for the last two thousand years had not been developing with any consideration of His teaching. In what sense did Jewish tradition belong to us, who looked to His authority? And in what sense did His teaching belong to Jewish tradition, which had not accepted His authority for two thousand years?

A prime example of this problem concerns the Lord's Prayer. While there is a great deal of debate in Messianic and Jewish-studies circles about the original purpose of this prayer, the theory that gained the most traction among Orthodox Messianics online is that it was originally intended as a concluding prayer for the Amidah. A number of such prayers circulated in late antiquity, before most Jewish communities settled on a prayer called the *Elohai Netzor*, "My God, the Keeper". However, these same Messianic communities were generally unwilling to replace the Elohai Netzor with the Lord's Prayer (the *Avinu* in Hebrew). The community of Israel had settled on the Elohai Netzor, and that was that. Consensus is one of the highest legal principles in this tradition. But how were we to claim we were Messianic if we neglected the Messiah's, the Son of God's, own halakha, His legal tradition? And if we were to give Him precedence, in what sense were we following the Tradition?

Many preferred to view the Our Father as a summary of the Amidah. This places Yeshua closer to the heart of traditional Judaism because it means that when His disciples asked Him how to pray, He answered, "Pray the Amidah." And it solved the legal problem. It was an extremely attractive solution, the only problem being that it did not seem to be true at all. The similarities between the two were superficial and were better explained by saying that they shared a general, Second Temple Judaism milieu.

I continued to struggle with these questions all semester, and in December I took a step toward processing this problem. At the end of my sophomore year, I was beginning to think about what would come after college. I did not think I was at all prepared to be a member of the clergy because I did not have a pastoral bone in my body, but I also did not think there would be a place for me in the academy. Writing seemed a possible alternative, to pursue my academic bent and enrich the theology of my community, without attempting to be a rabbi. As a first sally into this world, I began a blog.

The blog was specifically dedicated to questions of practice, of halakha, and I cheekily named it using a Karl Marx quote, *Nothing to Lose but Your Shackles*. I had great ambitions about guest writers and daily portions of Scripture in addition to the weekly posts about halakha, but only my own halakha posts ever really materialized, in part because of my commitment to classes.

Most of these posts were not profound or revelatory, but they were not supposed to be. In many cases, they were simply collocating the teaching of Yeshua on a given subject with those of the Mishnah and the Talmud. In one post, I found that the Mishnah (Nedarim 9:1) actually agreed with Yeshua against the first-century Pharisees when it came to making oaths and taking care of one's parents (see Mt 15:4–6). Whereas the Pharisees said that anyone who makes a vow to give something to the Temple is not obligated to use that same thing to take care of his parents, Yeshua treated this as a perversion of the Law. As it turns out, Rabbi Eliezer makes an exception to oaths, saying they are annulled if one discovers that the promised items are needed by one's parents.

I kept up the blog until the spring of 2012, exploring a specifically Messianic halakha, which clung closely to the rabbinic tradition but would not compromise or neglect the teachings of Yeshua, even though I did not consistently incorporate the Lord's Prayer as a conclusion to the Amidah.

There is one odd thing about this blog to which I should draw the reader's attention. On the right-hand side was a list of suggested reading. It was typical of my emerging practice at the time that I no longer trusted most Hebrew Roots and Messianic sources, with select exceptions, such as First Fruits of Zion. I was making my own way somewhere in between Christianity and Judaism and preferred to alternate reading a traditional Jewish text and a Christian text. As a result, one of the top recommendations on the reading list was *Orthodoxy*, by G.K. Chesterton. I remember reading it in my apartment at Baylor, unable to tear myself away to do homework. I likely would never have picked up the copy I found in a secondhand bookstore if it hadn't been mentioned in *20 The Countdown Magazine*'s tribute to Rich Mullins as one of his favorites.

Orthodoxy is a fantastic combination of reason and mysticism, a moving faith in the Messiah, and an appeal to tradition as "the living faith of the dead", as opposed to "the dead faith of the living". Chesterton takes the axe to modern prejudices against miracles and against Christian tradition because they are, as he points out, nothing more than prejudices. He outlines his great case for traditional Christianity as a case for sanity, noting that the main difference between Christianity and the rest of the world is that the one is sane and the other is always at least a little insane. But it is not just a case for Christianity; it is a case for the Church. The chapter "The Paradoxes of Christianity" is particularly deadly in its humor; in it, Chesterton points out that the critics of Christianity endlessly contradict themselves: they accuse Christianity of being too pacifist and too violent, too puritanical and too luxurious, too fat and too thin. He concludes that "if Christianity was wrong, it was very wrong indeed." It was almost supernaturally wrong—unless it was supernaturally right and all these accusations, that it was wrong in a thousand ways, had more to do with its critics, who were misshapen in a thousand ways:

> Suppose we heard an unknown man spoken of by many men. Suppose we were puzzled to hear that some men said he was too tall and some too short; some objected to his fatness, some lamented his leanness; some thought him too dark, and some too fair. One explanation (as has already been admitted) would be that he might be an odd

> shape. But there is another explanation. He might be the right shape. Outrageously tall men might feel him to be short. Very short men might feel him too tall.... Perhaps, after all, it is Christianity that is sane and all its critics that are mad—in various ways.[9]

As one of those critics of traditional Christianity, I quailed. I told Lance, my Anglican seminarian friend, "If I can read that and not become a Catholic, it's either because I'm a genius or just too stubborn to admit when I'm wrong." He helpfully reminded me that I'm not a genius.

I remember somewhere around this time mentioning offhand to a friend from home that I thought that, fundamentally, Catholicism was closer to the truth than Protestantism was because it had this faith in Tradition, as well as practices such as prayer for the dead. He was taken aback but was not able to give a specific reason he felt I was wrong; he only insisted that Protestants had at least tried to get rid of all the pagan accretions that Catholics retained. But we did not accept that they had been successful, so that seemed like much of a muchness to me.

I continued attending the Conservative synagogue, but something was beginning to change in me. I took Lance with me once, and he told me I should visit an Orthodox church. "Everything they do is symbolic. You have that bobbing thing [he meant shuckling], but every part of what they do is a symbol." I was annoyed and ignored him. But soon, when I was praying at the synagogue on a Sabbath morning, I felt the overwhelming desire to cross myself. I had no theological or halakhic justification for making the sign of the cross, but when

[9] G.K. Chesterton, *Orthodoxy: The Romance of Faith* (1908; repr., Peabody, Ma.: Hendrickson Publishers, 2006), 84–86.

we prayed for the coming of the Messiah in the Amidah, the desire came over me with such force that I sobbed because I was unable to make this simple gesture to honor the great Rabbi. I did not know what to do with that experience. Mom had described a similar experience she had had years before when visiting an Episcopal church where George Washington prayed. She said, "I almost felt compelled to cross myself." At the time, I dismissed what she said with a roll of my eyes, but now it was happening to me. I did not tell anyone because it disturbed me. I was not supposed to want to make the sign of the cross. I was supposed to have the richer tradition, the one closer to the Messiah Himself. So why did this feel like a wedge between Him and me? Why did I ache?

12

During the summer of 2011, I studied German in Berlin, but little theological development happened there. I visited Warsaw after finishing the summer semester in Berlin and prayed at the only house of worship that survived WWII—the Nożyk Synagogue. I have fond memories of the trip, but none that concern our present purposes. I did reasonably well in class, but my German was, and remains, very poor.

The fall brought an exciting slate of classes, including a Hebrew Readings class on Chronicles, a class on the Prophets, and Cross-Cultural Linguistics, but also a new challenge. I have no memory of how I met Isaac, but he was immediately enthusiastic when he discovered that there was another Messianic on campus. He was studious, energetic, and fundamentalist. I struggled to have a conversation with him, but we prayed together, and that was a salve. He got us into chapels on campus to pray with a few other students who, themselves charismatics and Evangelicals, were interested in Jewish traditions. It was a looser approach to traditional Jewish prayer, but I decided to prioritize fellowship, at least at times, over the details of prayer practice. These were very good people, and I was not deserving of their company, and, to this day, they do not know what happened next.

As the High Holy Days of the fall approached, they wanted to know what my plans were, and I told them I was going to go to the synagogue. They asked to come along, and I, with some reservations, agreed to drive them all so that we could pray together. After the service for Rosh Hashanah, there was a celebratory meal. One of my friends began to speak French with a member of the synagogue seated at our table, and I wandered off to get seconds. At some point, the subject of Yeshua came up. I was not aware this had happened.

When I returned the next Sabbath for prayer, the rabbi took me into his office, told me what had happened, and disinvited me from the synagogue. I apologized profusely and left, devastated. I had lost the only consistent community of prayer I had, and I returned to my apartment feeling defeated and alone.

So I refocused on this little ragtag band of people who wanted to learn about Jewish prayer. They were exceedingly loving and encouraging, and I did not hold anything against them. To be honest, I felt guilty. Yeshua said we would be thrown out of the synagogues (see Jn 16:2), but I did not even have the courage to be thrown out on my own account. The others in the group all attended churches, though, and I was uniquely dependent upon our irregular meetings. Attending a synagogue where I rarely spoke to people was a little alienating, but this was worse.

This situation persisted through the spring semester of 2012, but with two new developments, one exciting to me and the other frustrating and disappointing. Dr. Nogalski offered a course in Biblical Poetry that semester, which sounded delightfully challenging. One of the required course texts was *The Idea of Biblical Poetry* by my hero, James Kugel. Another of the required texts, which I enjoyed less but which proved an important catalyst, was Adele Berlin's *The Dynamics of Biblical Parallelism*. It was as challenging a class as I had hoped, and the texts were quite difficult, coming primarily from Jeremiah. Hebrew was not a prerequisite for the class, but it was better if you could work in Hebrew.

My eyes were opened to the tropes and organization of poetry in the Hebrew Bible. Kugel describes the poetic line in Hebrew as a couplet, a single sentence in two clauses in the form "A, what is more, B". The psalms, which I loved so much, had new clarity for me. What had seemed strange repetitions now stood out in three dimensions as parallel lines, each adding something unique to the whole thought. One of my earliest struggles with the Bible was finally being resolved. I had been reading the psalms and attempting to understand them, with some success, for years, but now they opened up with profound clarity.

Adele Berlin attempted to explain by linguistic means places in poetic texts that lacked parallelism. I have so far kept this work away from technical issues, but that will become increasingly difficult from here on. I must address this topic somewhat technically, but I will try to keep from going too far into the weeds. In cases where a line appeared to lack parallelism, Berlin resolved this problem by appealing to a theory developed by Noam Chomsky called the universal grammar hypothesis. Chomsky's idea is that all languages are based on a limited number of grammatical possibilities, and one of the corollaries of this theory is that the grammar of a sentence as it appears, the "surface structure", is undergirded by a "deep structure" and that some elements of the sentence have been secondarily moved from their original "deep structure" positions to their "surface structure" positions. Sentences are originally formulated in the mind according to their deep structure and then undergo "movement" of some elements to reach the form of the sentence as actually spoken.[1] Berlin hypothesized that parallel lines that do not have similar grammar on the surface level would have it on the level of deep structure.[2]

This theory struck me as entirely fascinating—and also entirely wrong. This "movement" is subconscious, if it is real at all,[3] and so not available for a poet to use in making parallelism. In what was supposed to be a book report on *The Dynamics of Biblical Parallelism*, I proposed that we could instead use a theory I had learned about in linguistics to explain these nonparallel lines. The philosopher of language Paul Grice proposed that we have rules of conversation about how we communicate—things like "always say what you believe to be true" and "always give enough information". But violations of these rules do not always result in a complete failure in the communication; in fact, they usually result in an indirect meaning.[4] If I say something that I obviously cannot possibly believe to be true, such as "I *love* it when people make my work harder", my conversation partner easily interprets this as sarcasm. I proposed that this theory could be applied to lines of poetry that lacked parallelism: that they genuinely did not conform to the rule because they were doing something else, what Grice called *flouting* the rule.

[1] For a good introduction to the principles of the universal grammar hypothesis, see Frank Heny, "Syntax: The Structure of Sentences", in *Language: Introductory Readings*, 7th ed., ed. Virginia Clark, Paul Eschholz, et al. (New York: Bedford/St. Martins, 2008), 191–231.

[2] Adele Berlin, *The Dynamics of Biblical Parallelism*, revised and expanded edition, Biblical Resource Series, ed. Astrid B. Beck and David Noel Freedman (Grand Rapids, Mich.: William B. Eerdmans, 2008), 56–63.

[3] And there is significant evidence that it is not, but the reasons are far too technical to discuss here.

[4] For a summary, see Peter Grundy, *Doing Pragmatics*, 2nd ed. (New York: Oxford University Press, 2000), 70–100; or Paul Grice, *Studies in the Way of Words* (Cambridge, Ma.: Harvard University Press, 1991).

While I was doing this exciting academic work, I was still plagued by the problem of Messianic identity, specifically for those of us who were of Gentile origin, and it complicated my search for how we related to Jewish tradition. First Fruits of Zion threw its hat into the ring, at first discussing an idea and then publishing a white paper titled *The Divine Invitation*. FFOZ's idea was that all remained as before with regard to the Torah: Gentiles were saved as Gentiles and Jews as Jews, and their responsibilities were distinct. However, God had given an invitation to the believing Gentiles to participate in the Torah life, without obligating them to it. This might mean partial observance or a very complete observance, but still as Gentiles, as Saint Paul suggested in 1 Corinthians 7.

Remember my requirements for a theory of the community, as stated in chapter 7:

1. It had to include a robust view of the union of Jews and Gentiles in alignment with Saint Paul's tearing down "the dividing wall" and "neither Jew nor Greek" claims.
2. It had to make sense of the claim that some native branches of Israel had been removed to make way for the Gentiles and that this was the result of the gospel.
3. There had to be no second-class citizens, as all are "fellow citizens with the saints, and of the household of God" (Eph 2:19).
4. It had to be not merely theoretical but practical, extending to very concrete matters regarding table fellowship and the sharing of food (see Gal 2:12–14).
5. It had to allow for the prophet Isaiah's claim that the Gentiles would observe the same Sabbath as the Jews and would be required to celebrate the feast of Tabernacles at the Temple (see Is 56:6; Zech 14:16–19).

6. It could not involve hypothetical reconstructions and re-forming the evidence to suit our preconceived theology.

FFOZ's proposal struck me as little better than a "two covenant" solution and inherently unworkable. But for a long time, I avoided reading the paper. I did not want to read it because the premise was flawed, and I dreaded the possibility that our best minds had failed to provide a meaningful solution to the problem that loomed largest in my theology.

At the same time, I began digging into Christian scholarship, especially the work of E. P Sanders and N. T. Wright, and I was appalled by what I found: they were familiar with the Jewish roots of Christianity, and they had accounted for them. This was not supposed to be possible. A bishop in the Church of England was not supposed to have a context for the Jewishness of Jesus, let alone the Jewishness of Paul. The implicit premise I had heard over and over again in the Hebrew Roots Movement was that if the Christians only knew what we knew, they would agree with us. But N. T. Wright and, very shortly thereafter, Pope Benedict XVI (of all people!) obstinately remained Christian despite knowing at least as much as I did about Jesus the Jew.

About this time, Lance invited me to hear him preach at the local Anglican mission. He had gone to synagogue with me, so I felt I owed it to him to return the favor. I have reason to think this might have happened in the fall of 2010, not the spring of 2011, but I am uncertain. The mission met in a church building that was owned by a charity. The sanctuary was still mostly intact, but the pews had been removed and the room was carpeted. The windows, neo-Gothic arches only lightly bordered in patterned stained glass, shone clear. Folding chairs were arranged in an oval in the middle of the floor, with a small pinewood table at one end. The priest, Father Michael, was a lanky, thickly accented Texan with a glorious goatee.

Lance introduced me to Father Michael, who then excused himself and returned a moment later in a long white robe unlike anything I had seen a Christian wearing before. I was taken aback because I recognized it in spirit, if not exactly in style. He was dressed as a priest. As much as I knew that Christianity has a long history, it was to me essentially something modern and unconnected to the world of ancient Israel. I was accustomed to pastors dressed in modern clothes, ranging from the conservative suit and tie to the hip khakis and polos, singing songs written from the eighteenth century onward in services without a hint of antiquity. But here was a priest dressed as a priest. Little did I know that this garment was the much-maligned cassock-alb; to me, it was the white *kutonet*, the tunic of priests in Aaron's lineage. The liturgy was a stripped-down affair, and the music was accompanied by guitar. It was simple but beautiful. It was as clear as light and suffused with the text of Sacred Scripture. I was deeply uncomfortable—and deeply impressed.

Lance never tried to convert me, which would not have worked anyway. He just showed me the wealth of his tradition and let me figure it out for myself. I began tentatively to learn about the apostolic churches and their traditions and what they might provide as a solution to my problem of Tradition.

I began, on occasion, to attend services at the Anglican mission. Once my guard had come down and I saw that this was neither the irreverent Evangelical worship I knew nor what I still assumed would be idolatrous Catholic worship, my reticence about attending a church, at least occasionally, evaporated. The mission soon acquired and began meeting in a house in downtown Waco. The services remained simple, with the music usually accompanied by guitar—quiet, traditional nineteenth-century hymns, most of them familiar to me from my Baptist days. There was also a student pursuing a master's degree in music who liked to bring his hammered dulcimer from time to time. The hammered dulcimer was particularly beloved of Rich Mullins, a virtuoso of the instrument, because it connected him to his heritage in Appalachia. I loved the sound of that dulcimer as it accompanied the simple spoken liturgy that they prayed from printouts. I was uncomfortable with my own attendance there, but the liturgy was biblical and, despite being disconnected from every other community I had, this community was welcoming, supportive, and intellectual.

On April 25, 2012, I wrote my last blog entry on *Nothing to Lose but Your Shackles*. It was about martyrdom and capital punishment and the connection between them in Jewish law. Then I went home for the summer and dove into E. P. Sanders' magisterial *Paul and Palestinian Judaism*. Sanders extensively records the traditions and theologies of the Jewish groups who lived at the time of Yeshua and Paul in order to put Paul in his first-century context. I was tormented by these problems of our relationship to the Jewish people and Jewish tradition, and I did not see a systematic way forward, so I hoped to gain clarity from Sanders' research.

Then, sometime in August, the two authors of *The Divine Invitation* came to Beit HaDerekh to present their thesis. I went with my hopes high but strained. The presentation failed to convince me at all. It had been, in many ways, my last hope for the Messianic movement. Once again, their thesis was that Jewish believers had an *obligation* to observe the Law of Moses in its entirety, according to historical Jewish tradition, while the Gentiles had only an *invitation* to join, to one extent or another, in those observances. Gentiles were left with a tradition that they were obligated to believe but not obligated to observe, and while these authors insisted that this did not make Gentiles second-class citizens, that insistence rang hollow. They explained that Saint Paul's theology of the Law was about allowing Gentiles into the fullness of the relationship with God without requiring them to observe the Torah. This means that the Torah was no longer an obstacle to Gentiles' being joined to the People of God.

This view required such a tortured interpretation of Ephesians 2, though, that it was immediately untenable to me. I knew that Paul wrote that we were formerly called Gentiles according to the flesh and foreigners to the commonwealth of Israel and were now brought near in Christ, who destroyed "the dividing wall" between us and abolished "in his flesh the law of commandments and ordinances" (Eph 2:14–15, RSV-2CE) so that we could be one new man. I went home with a conviction: a tradition was necessary for understanding the Bible, and we did not have one. The only one that I could see was in the apostolic churches. The next morning, I rose early, drove to the local Catholic bookstore, which I had never been in before, and bought a Catholic prayer book.

The book was a one-week devotional of Saint Clare, but it was the only one I could find. I still had my Book of Common Prayer, but I was unsure how to use it, and besides, I had left it in Waco. I remember the day I left to return to Baylor for my final semester in August 2012. Just before I got in the car, Mom asked something to the effect of "So, is that it?"

"That's it", I said. "I don't know what church I'm going to join, but it's got to be the Orthodox, the Anglicans, or the Catholics."

Part IV

Canterbury (2012–2015)

13

When I returned to Waco in late summer of 2012, it was not yet obvious which communion I would choose. I knew very little about any of them except that they all had bishops and claimed apostolic succession, which was the main thing I was seeking. Apostolic succession meant both the continuity with antiquity, guaranteed by Judaism's "unbroken chain of succession", and missing in the Messianic movement, and also the source of an authoritative tradition of biblical interpretation.

In the spring of 2012, I had begun a second blog, *Counting to Infinity*, to discuss theology and mysticism and to share some of my poetry. While I mothballed *Nothing to Lose but Your Shackles*, I continued posting on this other blog, and upon returning to Waco in August, I explained my new change. It was a short post, so I will share it here in full:

> *Lord, have mercy on me, a sinner.*
>
> I'm leaving the Messianic movement and joining the Eastern Orthodox Church. I thought I owed everyone an explanation as to why I am making this change. I have long maintained that Scripture cannot stand on its own. We require a Tradition. We need a Tradition to tell us what books belong in the Bible, in which version, and how to interpret the Bible. In the Messianic movement, we've seen what happens when we don't have this. Ever since Monte Judah threw Hebrews out of the canon and Michael Rood started using the Shem Tov Matthew, the

foundation of our idea of "what makes up the Bible" has been shaken. Someone has to have the authority to say that XYZ belongs and ABC does not.

This is why we have apostolic succession. The Messiah gave legal authority to the Apostles when He said, "Whatever you bind on earth will be bound in heaven and whatever you loose on earth will be loosed in heaven." This authority has been passed on continuously through the apostolic succession, and it is by this same authority that the Church has told us what belongs in the Bible, and what it means. Without this authority, we have no way to know what is genuinely "the Bible" and what is not. Is the Church of the East correct to reject 2 Peter, 2–3 John, Jude, and Revelation? Are the Nazarenes right to use only the Hebrew Matthew? Was Luther right to reject James? Why do we use the Apocalypse of John, and not the Apocalypse of Peter? How do we know that John is in agreement with the Synoptic Gospels? The answer to all of these is Church Tradition. Given the canon, it is not too difficult to defend Messianic ideas, but it is also not difficult to defend Orthodox Christianity. The question, then, is how do we decide between two positions that we can defend from the same text, and how do we know that we have the right text? We know that we have the right text because of the authority of the Church, and we understand how to interpret it because we have inherited its interpretation in an unbroken line of apostolic succession. I realize that this will come as quite a surprise to some of you; some of you have seen it coming. What I hope most of all is that you will continue in steadfast devotion to the Messiah of Israel and the world.

Even though I did not yet understand the justification for traditional Christianity's relationship to the Torah, my conversion was based not on my personal ability to answer such questions but on my personal inability to do so. As a result, I did not hesitate to change my life completely. I immediately took off my yarmulke and my tallit katan, stopped observing the Sabbath, and stopped praying from the Siddur. I remember feeling exposed without my tallit katan and my kippah and vulnerable without the rituals and traditions that had occupied me at every hour of the day. I did not even know how to pray over my food anymore because after the *berakhot*, the traditional blessings of Judaism, the kind of spontaneous meal prayers of my childhood Baptist days felt incredibly hollow. Losing my rituals felt like losing my identity, which they established, and I did not yet have a Christian identity to replace them. I was naked and alone, like a newborn baby.

The year before, I had dropped my Biblical Languages major because fulfilling the language requirements proved almost impossible for me. I was now a Linguistics major with a Religion minor, and I had fulfilled my language requirements with four semesters of Hebrew, two of Greek, two of German, and one of Old English. I was thus free to explore theology more broadly, and two classes during that last semester proved extremely formative: History of Eastern Orthodoxy and The Oxford Christians, the latter taught by the legendary Flannery O'Connor scholar Professor Ralph Wood.

To the complete novice, of the three communions—the Orthodox, the Anglican, and the Catholic—it is Eastern Orthodoxy that presents itself as the most ancient and traditional in appearance, so I naturally pursued that avenue first. The liturgy, doctrines, and garments of Orthodoxy have remained essentially unchanged for more than a thousand years, and Orthodoxy is rooted in the East Mediterranean world of early Christianity.

A mission of the Orthodox church based in Antioch, Syria, called the Antiochene Orthodox church, was just beginning to meet one Sunday evening a month at Holy Spirit Episcopal Church. I decided to pursue membership in this church because I thought it would be rooted in Semitic tradition, not realizing it was a thoroughly Greek Byzantine rite. Nothing about this church's Divine Liturgy was remotely familiar to me, and, as a result, I struggled to appreciate it. It had what I thought I was looking for—bishops who were descended in a direct line from the apostles through the laying on of hands in ordination, ancient apostolic traditions, ancient liturgy, and broad doctrinal agreement—but it was, at the time, all but completely inaccessible to me.

Because I had no church home and the location was familiar, I fell into attending Holy Spirit the remaining three Sundays each month. (While there was still an Anglican mission in Waco, it was not at this time meeting every week.) This was a very helpful opportunity to become familiar with the Book of Common Prayer.

Once the criterion of agreement with Jewish tradition was removed, the 1979 BCP struck me as graceful and biblical. The service I customarily attended at Holy Spirit was an early-morning Rite I (traditional) spoken liturgy, equivalent to a Catholic Low Mass—that is, without chanting or music. There were few attendees, and they did not often speak. When I arrived, the day was still young and the streets were quiet. I would slip in softly in the gray predawn and kneel in the quiet and listen to the silent voice of God. The priest, a retired army colonel, would enter, and his solemn voice would intone, "Blessed be God: Father, Son, and Holy Spirit." The basic outline of the service followed: praise in the form of one of the most ancient Christian hymns, the Gloria; then readings from Scripture; a sermon; the Creed; the Prayers of the People, which are intercessory prayers based on the Amidah; and the confession of sin. The service then transitioned from the Liturgy of the Word, with its roots in the synagogue service, to Holy Communion, which was ultimately derived, though I did not know it at the time, from the mealtime blessings of Second Temple Judaism. It began with thanksgiving and the "Holy, Holy, Holy" of Isaiah and Revelation. Then came the Last Supper narrative; the prayer for the blessing of the Holy Spirit, called the Epiclesis; the Lord's Prayer; and the breaking of the bread and distribution of Communion. It was all intensely biblical—and surprisingly familiar. The liturgy I knew had been re-formed for this Messiah-centered purpose, but in many of its essentials it was still the liturgy I knew. There was nothing remotely pagan, as I had been led to believe.[1]

The priest's favorite "sentence of comfort" after confession was 1 Timothy 1:15: "This is a true saying, and worthy of all men to be received, that Christ Jesus came into the world to save sinners"[2]—a word that haunted me and is now indelibly impressed upon my memory. It took a few weeks, but I became comfortable with the BCP, and this was a boon. I remained vulnerable, but I was no longer naked.

At Holy Spirit, the people received Communion while kneeling at the altar rail in holy meditation. Then they were blessed and dismissed, and some remained to pray while the rest filed out in holy silence. I did not know how

[1] See Mar Sharhad Yawsip Jammo, "The Chaldean Liturgy", in *Emmanuel: That Is, the Book of Public Prayer, Selected from the Yearly Cycle of the Hudra, with the Volume of Kahnayta, Which Is the Book of the Rites of All the Sacraments as Celebrated in the Chaldean Church of the East*, ed. Mar Sharhad Yawsip Jammo and Fr. Andrew Younan (San Diego: Chaldean Media Center, 2013), xix–xxxvii.

[2] Episcopal Church, *The Book of Common Prayer and Administration of the Sacraments and Other Rites and Ceremonies of the Church: Together with the Psalter or Psalms of David According to the Use of the Episcopal Church* (New York: Seabury Press, 1979), 332.

lucky I was to have this experience or how rare the reverential care of that service is. I did not know that silence in the liturgy is uncommon in the twenty-first century and that clunky, unpoetic modern translations are now the norm, in both Anglican and Catholic liturgies. It remains to me the sacred womb from which I was birthed back into Christendom.

Six days after posting that blog entry saying I was definitely going to join the Orthodox church, and already a catechumen, I posted again that I might actually join the Anglican church but that I had reservations. I was most concerned about its low sacramentology and the Thirty-Nine Articles' apparent affirmation of a doctrine of *prima scriptura*—that is, the idea that Scripture is the primary authority, if not the only one—when it states that Holy Scripture contains all things necessary to salvation (article VI). That statement alone did not necessarily exclude the possibility that it meant "Scripture as rightly interpreted in the light of Holy Tradition", but it did give me pause because this was practically the whole reason I had left the Messianic movement. If Tradition was not given some kind of veto in interpretation, then we were in the same position as the Messianics.

My prayer routine had become somewhat disorganized, but I prayed even more frequently. Though I still had a car, I took to walking back and forth between my apartment and campus so that I could pray the Rosary. I often replaced the Hail Mary with the traditional Orthodox Jesus Prayer: "Lord, Jesus Christ, Son of God, have mercy on me, a sinner." I did not yet have a theological framework for this kind of repetitive, meditative prayer and only just had a framework for the intercession of the saints and the Blessed Virgin, but I was entrusting myself to the Church and her prayer.

I did not yet know anything about the traditional Christian Liturgy of the Hours, or daily prayer, and it would be years before I really became acquainted with them. Lance gave me an assortment of Orthodox pamphlets and a prayer card that still sits on my desk. Among the pamphlets was the *Pocket Prayer Book for Orthodox Christians*, containing a short order for Morning and Evening Prayer, among other things, but they were exceedingly short and repetitious and unsatisfactory after the rich daily prayer tradition of Judaism. I must give this booklet full credit, however, for hammering home the trinitarian formulas and the Creed, which rehabilitated me from my nontrinitarian heresy. Morning Prayer began, "In the Name of the Father, and of the Son, and of the Holy Spirit" and proceeded to the Trisagion—"Holy God, Holy Mighty, Holy Immortal: Have mercy on us"—before introducing the Glory Be—"Glory be to the Father and to the Son and to the Holy Spirit: now and ever, and unto ages of ages. Amen." Then came the longer Troparia to the Holy Trinity and the Prayer to the Holy Trinity and the Creed. No one celebrates the Trinity like the Orthodox, and this prayer regimen, though I kept it only briefly, was the palate cleanser I needed to relearn this mystery.

The Daily Office of the BCP came much closer to fulfilling my longing for a daily liturgy. It was my Christian Siddur, and I began to carry my red misbound pew-back copy with me everywhere. It was centered on Holy Scripture and included a reasonable, if still somewhat small, proportion of psalms. More importantly, the canticles! Included were Pascha Nostrum, an ancient Christian hymn composed of Saint Paul's hymns from 1 Corinthians 5:7–8; 15:20–22 and Romans 6:9–11, and, from Luke 2, the Magnificat, Mary's song; the Benedictus, Zechariah's song; and the Nunc dimittis, Simeon's song—all the New Testament prayers I loved in Fisher's Siddur, besides the glorious Catholic tradition of the Apostles' Creed and the ancient Christian hymn *Phos hilaron*:

> O gracious Light,
> Pure brightness of the everliving Father in heaven,
> O Jesus Christ, holy and blessed!
>
> Now as we come to the setting of the sun,
> And our eyes behold the vesper light,
> We sing thy praises, O God: Father, Son, and Holy Spirit.
>
> Thou art worthy at all times to be praised by happy voices,
> O Son of God, O Giver of life,
> And to be glorified through all the worlds.[3]

I began what I would later describe as a "torrid love affair" with the book.[4] At times, I would pore over it when it was not an hour of prayer, simply because I loved it. It even made use of all the psalms, though it took three months to pray them all. A drawback was that it required me to carry a Bible as well. I was not in the habit of doing this because I usually had a Hebrew Bible or Old Testament class that necessitated carrying my Hebrew edition of the Old Testament, so adding a Bible on top was not particularly convenient.

I also remained uncomfortable with a number of things in the Thirty-Nine Articles. They were somewhat ambiguous, but it was clear to me that they were meant to defend

[3] Episcopal Church, *Book of Common Prayer*, 64.

[4] See Matthew D. Wiseman, "This Is Not a Project: Introduction", *The North American Anglican*, August 15, 2016, https://northamanglican.com/this-is-not-a-project-introduction.

a basically Lutheran or Reformed theology. I have been many things in my life, but I have never been Reformed, and I had no interest in becoming so. If I was interested in the Anglican Communion, it was because it seemed to be the heir of English Catholicism, and I wanted to keep far away from Protestantism, with its lack of belief in the authority of the Tradition.

I brought my concerns to the priest from the Anglican mission where Lance had preached in the spring. At the time, I was only vaguely aware of the Anglican-Episcopal schism, let alone the finer points of church politics. I did not know the difference between a church in the theologically diverse Anglican Church in North America and one in Rwanda's thoroughly Low Church, Evangelical Anglican Mission in America. Father Michael's was the latter. We sat down in his kitchen over drinks, and I raised my concerns, oblivious to the fact that he almost certainly took the opposite approach to mine and was probably more comfortable with an Evangelical interpretation of the Articles than with an Anglo-Catholic one. But he pastorally pointed out that the ambiguities I had noticed were deliberate, that the Articles had a long history and were in many ways a compromise between traditional Catholic and progressive Reformed factions in the church under the early Protestant monarchs Henry VIII and Elizabeth I.

I took Father Michael's words to the bank, and soon all my effort was focused on integrating into the Anglican community in Waco. I had stopped attending the Divine Liturgy of the Antiochene Orthodox church by September 5, according to my blog. In that blog post, I listed my reasons for my decision. I dismissed the papacy and the *Filioque* (the phrase "and the Son", which was added to the Nicene Creed in the Catholic West but not in the

Orthodox East) as well as Saint Augustine's theology of salvation as late Roman additions incompatible with the true faith, while at the same time blaming Eastern Orthodoxy's internal dissentions and the Messianic movement's absence of unifying authority. With no hint of irony, my reason for joining the Anglican Communion was that the Thirty-Nine Articles were open to interpretation, while my objection to Messianism was that, without authoritative Tradition, the Bible was open to interpretation.

Due to my natural inclination to make snap decisions and my impatience with deliberation, I felt more homeless than ever, and after so many years in a definite, if disorganized, community, I was not prepared for a long wait. I needed a community, and I already had close friends among the Anglicans and a clergyman I intuitively trusted. So I rushed in. At this time, the witness of John Henry Newman was already becoming important to me. In the mid-nineteenth century, after nearly two centuries of a deeply Protestant Anglicanism, Newman, along with his fellows Edward Pusey and John Keble, among others, began a High Church revival in Anglicanism, relying on the early Church Fathers and the High Church tradition of the Church of England under the House of Stuart—James I, James VI, and Charles I—and William Laud, who was Charles' archbishop of Canterbury. Together, they published a series of anonymous articles detailing their conservative, patristic, ritualist approach to Anglicanism called the *Tracts for the Times*. They and their supporters became known as the Oxford Movement, the founding revival of Anglo-Catholicism in modern times.

The day I definitively decided to join the Anglican Communion, I spent the morning and early afternoon in the Baylor library, poring over Newman's great Anglo-Catholic apology, Tract 90, which attempts a Catholic reading of the Thirty-Nine Articles. Satisfied by Newman's view, and only vaguely aware that Newman himself was not satisfied by it, I closed my laptop and told the friends I was sitting with, "That settles it. I'm going to be an Anglican."

The situation at the Anglican mission in Waco had somewhat changed, as I have mentioned, and Communion was celebrated only once a month, when a priest could come down from Fort Worth, the diocese now in charge. It was more student focused, and we met regularly on a weeknight in one of the chapels on campus to pray the Evening Office and hear a lecture on the Book of Common Prayer by Professor David Lyle Jeffrey. He would soon become a major influence on my understanding of literature and interpretation, especially through his magisterial work, *People of the Book*. His lectures were counted as catechesis—formal religious education—for those seeking Confirmation, emphasizing the centrality of the Book of Common Prayer to the Anglican tradition.

Meanwhile, in my History of Eastern Orthodoxy class, I had made a new friend, Emily. Emily was my first good Catholic friend. By the time we really got to know each other, I had landed on Anglicanism, but we were such kindred souls that we referred to each other as "Roman Twin" and "Anglican Twin". Because I felt as if I were learning the Bible all over again—words that I knew but with meanings that were completely novel—I leaned heavily on Emily and Lance as points of reference. I may be romanticizing my friendships in hindsight, but the way I remember it, Emily and I, along with her roommate, Amanda, were inseparable that year.

The class also gave me an opportunity to delve into the early Church Fathers and Orthodox theology, at least a little, without taking away from school time. For the first time, I began to learn what the Christians of the first four centuries believed and taught. I read the works of Justin Martyr, who lived less than a century after Christ, and Ignatius of Antioch, who was a personal student of the apostle John. And what they taught confirmed the conclusions I had already reached: that there was a body of Tradition and a system of church governance based on bishops who received their authority from the apostles.

The other class that impressed me deeply was The Oxford Christians. The class covered the Inklings (C. S. Lewis, J. R. R. Tolkien, and their informal literary society) alongside those who influenced them or associated with them but were not part of the group proper. Reading George MacDonald and C. S. Lewis felt like returning to my first love, and I could hardly believe that I got to read *The Lord of the Rings* and call it homework. It felt like getting away with something. The air was full of magic again and the crystal-clear light of liturgical silence. As with several other points, I feel I am neglecting many of the best people and the best friendships of the story, but suffice it to say, I made friends with outstanding people in that class.

One of those classmates deserves special recognition: Amy is a living saint, a true Catholic, and I truly feel I did not deserve her friendship. She introduced me to the importance of Saint Benedict and the motto *Ora et labora*—"Prayer and work"—one late night at Common Grounds over coffee. Though I did not pursue Saint Benedict or Benedictine life further at the time, Amy planted a seed that would lie dormant for several years before it began to sprout and grow. For that I owe her an immense debt.

Throughout the fall of 2012, Mom sent me a series of N. T. Wright's books, beginning with *Justification*, followed by *How God Became King* and *Surprised by Hope*. I considered these, together with a book on Father Austin Farrer, *The Truth-Seeking Heart*, which we read for The Oxford Christians, to be my crash course on Anglican theology. I began, for the first time, to read Saint Paul honestly and clearly and without an agenda. Even at the time, I did not always agree with the good bishop Wright, but I could not have had a more valuable tutor.

Near the end of September, I wrote a blog entry on justification in the Epistle to the Romans, trying to grapple with a new understanding of what the Torah was for and in what ways it had been changed in the New Covenant. I was, at the time, semi-Pelagian because, in accord with Jewish theology, I did not accept the idea of sin as a state of being. As far as I was concerned, we inherited only an inclination to sin, rather than a state of being sinful. Adam's death, not Adam's sin, was passed down. The understanding of Romans I expounded had problems, but it was a real beginning. In that blog entry, I wrote:

> The indication from the book of Hebrews is that it is a change from symbol to reality. I think I'm beginning to understand the symbol and reality. Standards designed to make a distinction between Jews and Gentiles existed to demonstrate the idea of holiness and the distinction between us and the world. These continue, but the change of status brings, by nature, a change in the realization of holiness and distinction. Saint John explains what these look like under Christ: "We know that we have passed out of death into life, because we love the brethren" (1 John 3:14a). The idea Saint Paul presents in Galatians that the law is a teacher can be explained in terms of Saint John's idea of the law of love: that the laws which make a distinction teach love, because they require unquestioning devotion. They required that we be willing to express our love by following instructions which did not necessarily make sense to the rational mind, expressed now thusly: "But if any one has the world's goods and sees his brother in need, yet closes his heart against him, how does God's love abide in him?" (1 John 3:17).

Nothing had really passed out of our observance of the Law; we had simply moved from the symbol to the reality. I would not know until years later that this exact position was expressed by Saint Jerome.

This idea would soon be developed further, but before that happened, I graduated from Baylor in December 2012. My childhood ambition to go unnoticed had seemingly persisted, and I finished a mere fraction of a grade point shy of cum laude: doing neither so well nor so poorly as to be noticed by much of anyone. I then sent out graduate school applications to most of the same schools I had looked at for my undergraduate degree. The only major addition was applying to an MLitt program at the University of St Andrews in Scotland.

I continued to live in Waco after graduating, out of dread of Midland, and while I waited to hear back from graduate programs, I took writing jobs that Dad sent me, in business news and petroleum. That January I moved to a new apartment, and in the process, I had a long conversation with the guy whose room I was taking, an acquaintance named Bruk. His family was from Ethiopia, and he was a devout member of one of the nondenominational churches in town. I made an offhand comment about Mark 10 and divorce, which was a holdover from my Messianic days. I took Christ's command to be essentially the stricter Jewish view, which allowed divorce but required a high standard of reason for the divorce, following the school of Rabbi Shammai. Bruk immediately shut me down. "That's not what He said. He said no divorce."

We left the matter unresolved that evening, but I was bothered, and I needed to do more digging. Based on my findings, I posted a lengthy blog entry in which I admitted not only that Bruk was correct but that, as a result, I had turned a new corner in my understanding of Christianity and the Torah. For Christmas, Mom and Dad had gotten me all three series of Cleveland Coxe's classic Writings of the Church Fathers, so my first stop was Saint John Chrysostom's homily on the parallel text in Matthew 19. The line that immediately leapt out at me was Chrysostom's statement that Christ's ruling was "by the manner of the creation, and by the manner of lawgiving".[5] That Christ here corrects the Torah according to the order of creation is perhaps not groundbreaking, but that Chrysostom viewed it as a matter of harmonization, not of contradiction, was enlightening.

Saint Chrysostom showed me that all the changes Christ and Saint Paul talk about in the Law have to do with appeals they make to the created order. In Acts 17, Saint Paul appeals to our shared Creator for the equality of Jews and Gentiles in the covenant. In Matthew 19, Christ appeals to the first family of Creation for the laws of marriage and divorce. In Mark 7, when Christ "declares all foods clean", He appeals to the nature of the human body as God created it. In Matthew 12, when Christ discusses the Sabbath, He explains not only that work on the Sabbath is permitted in exigent circumstances—because the Sabbath was created for man, not man for the Sabbath—but also that it is allowed in the Temple and is therefore allowed in His presence because He is greater than the Temple. The Law was in some way being corrected on the basis of the created order.

This last point requires some elaboration because, over the following years, it would begin to loom the largest of

[5] John Chrysostom, Homily LXII on Matt. XIX, 1, in *The Homilies of St. John Chrysostom, Archbishop of Constantinople, on the Gospel of St. Matthew*, trans. George Prevost, rev. M.B. Riddle, vol. 10 of A Select Library of the Christian Church: Nicene and Post-Nicene Fathers, First Series, ed. Philip Schaff (Peabody, Ma.: Hendrickson Publishers, 1994), 381–86.

these examples in my mind. The Temple is laden with more symbolism than I can possibly explain. Philo, the ancient Jewish philosopher from Alexandria, describes it as a microcosm, a little universe.[6] Other mystics describe it as a body, with the Holy of Holies at its head. Holy places are places where the rules change; they are places of contact between life and death, between this world and the next. In the Old Testament, contacts with the holy are nearly always accompanied by what Kugel describes as "a moment of confusion": the prophet or patriarch starts off thinking that the person speaking is merely human, and then a confused moment of revelation follows, when the person is overwhelmed and unclear on what manner of encounter this is, before God makes it clear that this is a divine encounter and gives the revelation.[7] It is a bewildering, topsy-turvy encounter. One of the effects of this holiness is that the ordinary rules are often inverted, as when Christ explains to the apostles that in order to ascend, you must voluntarily descend. Saint Benedict even ties this fact to Jacob's ladder, on which we ascend by descending.[8]

In the Temple, the priests were not only *allowed* to perform tasks that were considered work and therefore normally forbidden on the Sabbath, but they were *required* to do work in order to carry out the service of the sanctuary. This permission and requirement were both effected by the presence of God: the service had to go forward in order to honor God even on the day of rest, and the

[6] See Philo Judaeus, *Special Laws I*, 12–17, *The Works of Philo: Complete and Unabridged*, trans. C.D. Yonge (Peabody, Ma.: Hendrickson Publishers, 1993), 534–67.

[7] James Kugel, *The God of Old: Inside the Lost World of the Bible* (New York: Free Press, 2003), 5–36.

[8] Timothy Fry, O.S.B., ed., *RB 1980: The Rule of St. Benedict in Latin and English with Notes* (Collegeville, Minn.: Liturgical Press, 1981), 192–93.

presence of divine holiness in the sanctuary made it permissible. It inverted the rules. So, in the very incarnate presence of the all-holy God, the rule was inverted even more so. He is the new Sanctuary of God's Glory. The Incarnation of the very creative Word meant a Divine Presence beyond that which came to Israel in the Temple, but it also meant a restoration of the created order. "If any one is in Christ, he is a new creation" (2 Cor 5:17). At the time, I imagined this to mean that there was some change to the Torah, but I would be corrected on that idea soon. What I rightly took from this is that the Torah remains substantially in place and that there is a definite system, based on the natural order, to its changes but that the "moral versus ceremonial" distinction—by which it is often said that the moral laws remain but the ceremonial laws have passed away—was not precise enough.

I therefore adopted an ancient theory of atonement called "recapitulation", which hinges on the idea of the new creation. When the Creator entered His own creation, it was renewed and returned to "factory settings", as it were. This explained the arguments that Christ made from the "order of creation", in the words of Chrysostom. He came to make His creatures new by allowing us to die to the fallen creation and rise to the restored order through participation in His own death and Resurrection.

14

In February 2013, I was confirmed in the Anglican Church in North America, in the Diocese of Fort Worth, under the authority of Bishop Jack Iker, perhaps the staunchest Anglo-Catholic in the denomination. It was a natural thing in the Diocese of Fort Worth to think of Anglicanism as the English branch of the Catholic Church. Confirmation took place in a side chapel at Lakeshore Baptist Church, where the Anglican mission had begun meeting once a month, when Father Chris would come to town. It was a momentous day. Lance and his new bride, Danielle, were confirmed the same day, along with some other friends. I felt I had come in out of the cold.

At the same time, the heady days of my early experience of the Anglican mission were gone, and because the nearest parish in the diocese was an hour and a half away, I only occasionally attended there and usually communed at Holy Spirit Episcopal instead. I remained, in many ways, theologically isolated. While Holy Spirit itself was moderate to conservative, it belonged to the rapidly liberalizing Episcopal Church, from which the Anglican Church in North America had recently separated over the ordination as bishop of an openly practicing homosexual man. Even though this parish leaned more conservative than the denomination as a whole, the conflict between the two churches was pervasive.

That spring I read the first two volumes of Benedict XVI's *Jesus of Nazareth*, a revolutionary text for me.

His chapter on the Sermon on the Mount contains a large section on the Torah of the Messiah. He points to the foundational text of the Messianic movement, Matthew 5:17–19, and rather than shying from its affirmation of the Torah, he highlights it: "The intention is not to abolish, but to fulfill, and this fulfillment demands a surplus, not a deficit, of righteousness."[1]

The Torah of the Messiah is not an altogether new Torah; it is a rereading of the Law of Moses. Benedict XVI refers us to Jacob Neusner's book *A Rabbi Talks with Jesus*, in which the rabbi's conclusion is that Jesus has not taken anything away from the Torah but that He has added something: Himself.[2] When He introduces Himself as the Lawgiver, as the locus of Divine Presence, He becomes the center of a New Covenant with a New Israel around the Eighth Day of the week: the day of new beginnings. I told one of my roommates, "I think the best way I can explain it is that though Hebrews describes the mystery as 'a change of law', and that is correct because it is in the Bible, you could also say that the Torah was the only thing that didn't change; but when God entered creation to make it new, the whole world changed, and the Law stood still as the pivot in the middle of it."

God's eternal Law, His self-revelation, did not change, but everything else did, and as a result, the whole world's relationship to that Law changed. Nothing is abrogated, but nothing is unchanged—the "moral" commandments included. Just as "You shall not commit adultery" becomes "Every one who looks at a woman lustfully has already committed adultery with her in his heart" (Mt 5:27–28),

[1] Joseph Ratzinger [Pope Benedict XVI], *Jesus of Nazareth: From the Baptism in the Jordan to the Transfiguration*, trans. Adrian J. Walker (New York: Image, 2007), 102.

[2] Ibid., 103–6.

deepening and transforming the morality of the Torah, Christ also declares Himself to be "greater than the temple" (Mt 12:6), transforming the whole sacrificial cultus of the Temple into the Sacrifice of the Mass. No part of the Torah was lost, and no part of it was untouched. The Torah had become the New Torah of Jeremiah 31.

Here, at last, in the heart of the Catholic Church, was the answer I had been seeking for ten years. It had been here all along, but I had taken the longest possible way to find it. My parents soon followed their children out of the Messianic movement and joined their local Anglican parish. Mom would later say, "I think it was God's work that we went through Messianism, because as Baptists we never would have looked into Tradition. We might have been very happy Baptists all our lives had the Messianic movement not taught us about our need for Tradition." The whole journey had been leading to this.

Though Ratzinger (Benedict XVI) immediately became the foundation of my understanding of the Gospel, the whole New Testament, and, very shortly thereafter, the liturgy and the Church, I did not convert to Catholicism. I still believed that the Anglican Communion was the Catholic Church for the English-speaking world. It was going to take something else to shake me loose from that belief.

Orthodoxy, tradition, and linguistics continued to be my main themes of meditation. I spent a great deal of time thinking about genre and the importance of rightly understanding a text's genre and its context to interpret it correctly. In the linguistic theories I was hoping to pursue in graduate school, specifically the approach known as "speech-act theory", the setting and genre of a speech or text is indispensable to its meaning. I was still rereading the Bible, and everything in it felt entirely new, and yet it resonated with all I had learned in my Messianic years. I was experiencing in microcosm the New Covenant—nothing had been lost, but everything had been gained, and the old came with me, but renewed. The idea of the Zecher, the memorial that counts as fulfilling a commandment, especially the sacrifices, was transformed into *metanoia*, the "memorial" of Luke 22:19. But, in traditional Christianity, the memorial was not a mere divine fiat; salvation was not present in Communion in any genealogical or arbitrary way. In the words of the *Catechism of the Catholic Church*, "In the New Testament, the memorial takes on new meaning. When the Church celebrates the Eucharist, she commemorates Christ's Passover, and it is made present: the sacrifice Christ offered once for all on the cross remains ever present [cf. Heb 7:25–27]. 'As often as the sacrifice of the Cross by which "Christ our Pasch has been sacrificed" is celebrated on the altar, the work of our redemption is carried out' [*LG* 3; cf. 1 Cor 5:7]" (1364).

The sacrifice of Christ is actually present, and the liturgy has made this clear from the beginning: "May the Lord accept the sacrifice at your hands ... for our good and the good of all his holy Church."[3] The entire sacrificial system lives, renewed and transformed, in this sacrifice, but it was not simply offered in the past; it was offered in eternity: the one sacrifice offered truly, every day. It is not a substitute, nor is it simply spiritual or historical; it is *real*, and it is heavenly.

This understanding of Communion had been a growing conviction of mine. Some understanding of the Real Presence of Christ in the Eucharist was universal to the historical traditions of Christianity, including not only the Anglicans but even the Lutherans. It was the Bible itself

[3] *The Roman Missal* (Totowa, N.J.: Catholic Book Publishing Corp., 2011), 382.

that convinced me to adopt the strongest possible version of this doctrine. The classic text in this discussion is John 6, in which the Messiah says several times things like "I am the bread of life; he who comes to me shall not hunger, and he who believes in me shall never thirst" (v. 35) and "I am the living bread which came down from heaven; if any one eats of this bread, he will live for ever; and the bread which I shall give for the life of the world is my flesh" (v. 51). But reading the chapter as a whole adds to the argument because it begins with the Feeding of the Five Thousand, so the subsequent discussion is about bread and what is true food, as opposed to mere bread. In verse 52, his hearers discuss among themselves the fact that He cannot mean what He says literally, and at that point, He answers with extraordinary clarity: "Truly, truly, I say to you, unless you eat the flesh of the Son of man and drink his blood, you have no life in you.... For my flesh is food indeed, and my blood is drink indeed. He who eats my flesh and drinks my blood abides in me and I in him" (vv. 53, 55–56).

For the first time in years, I thought about an argument I had with a Catholic student from the online academy where I took Norse Mythology. She mentioned this text, and I answered, "Sure, but Yeshua speaks in parables all the time." To which she answered, "Yeah, but He never says, 'This is the parable of Transubstantiation.'" She was right. Not only did He not call it a parable, but when asked about whether it was a metaphor, He doubled down. And as a result, many of His followers left (see v. 66). In fact, His answer to them did not sound like anything from the parables, but it did sound distinctly like His answer about divorce in Matthew 19:11. In both cases, He said that not everyone is able to receive His teaching. He seemed to mean this thing about His flesh being bread just as concretely as He meant the other one about divorce and remarriage.

Over the next year, I became deeply interested in Saint Paul's teaching on the same subject in 1 Corinthians 11—a text to which I had never paid serious attention. In verse 27, he makes the very serious claim that anyone who eats of the Bread or drinks of the cup unworthily "is guilty of profaning the body and blood of the Lord". But Saint Paul goes further, saying that some of the Corinthians had done so, and as a result they were physically ill or had even died (v. 30). Far from backing off, the entire New Testament seemed to make the strongest claims possible for the reality, the literalness even, of Christ's Presence in Communion.

In May, I received an acceptance letter from Duke University's M.A. program in Religious Studies, and shortly thereafter, I embarked on a late graduation trip to Scotland and Ireland with Mom and Dad and my maternal grandmother, Granny Ann. (By this time, Melody had married her college boyfriend, Brad, and they did not go.) The trip was short, lasting only ten days, and was unseasonably cold, even for Scotland, nearly the whole time. It was theologically uneventful for me, but I did have my first experience of St Andrews.

A friend from Baylor, Hank, was studying abroad there, and I tried to make plans with him ahead of time, but getting ahold of him was difficult. When we took the train up from Edinburgh for the day, though, I happened to bump into him on the street. Those familiar with the town will not be terribly surprised by the coincidence: the old town is quite small, and when living there, one almost constantly runs into friends and acquaintances. I stayed in Hank's dorm room for a night so he could show me the town, the university, and his friends.

On Sunday, I attended Communion at a Scottish Episcopal church near our bed-and-breakfast while the rest of the family went to the old High Kirk of the presbyterian Church of Scotland, St Giles. I assumed I would be familiar with the service, but I knew nothing, and really still know nothing to this day, about the service books commonly used in the United Kingdom since 2000 and how much they differ from the 1979 Book of Common Prayer, with which I was familiar, and even from the traditional 1662 book. It was a baffling experience more than anything. The church was a solemn Gothic Revival building, which inspired a sense of reverence, but once the liturgy began and I was fumbling with books and hymnals, I lost the ability to focus. After the service, a very kind woman took pity on me and guided me through the labyrinthine passages to the undercroft for coffee hour, where she expressed surprise at learning there were Anglicans anywhere outside Great Britain.

From Edinburgh we left for Dublin, where we stayed on the southern outskirts of the city for three days. The sun finally emerged on our last full day, just in time for Dad and me to climb Bray Head and take a few pictures. The stay was much too short to be particularly significant. It was an excellent time, and I regret terribly that I have not yet had an opportunity to go back to Ireland.

Scotland and Ireland in ten days together survives in my mind only in flashes. Just below the castle overlooking the New Town of Edinburgh was a tea shop where I liked to sit and watch the rain fall, and, in its little courtyard, the Writers' Museum with a fantastical collection of Burns, Scott, and Stevenson. In Dublin, there was a pub that I could not find again if my life depended on it; I spent a wet afternoon there reading over a pint of cider and a pile of bangers and mash. And, of course, I saw the magical Book of Kells exhibit at Trinity College. At a bookshop, I acquired an introductory Irish grammar and spent another afternoon in a tea shop at Bray familiarizing myself with it, but I have not since found the time to get much further than I did that day. The sheer speed of the trip meant that little else left more than a cold, gray impression of misty Romanticism.

Over the summer, I first visited, and then moved to, Durham, North Carolina, to begin working on my M.A. As with my friends at Baylor, I must here neglect a number of excellent teachers who were very important in teaching me to study the Hebrew Bible as an academic, but the growth of my theology at that time took place primarily outside the classroom. To avoid neglecting them entirely, I will simply mention here the deep debt that I owe especially to my advisor, Dr. Lieber, but also to all my professors there.

After finding the university on my first visit, I immediately went in search of the local Anglican parish, All Saints. One a little farther away was more to my aesthetic liking, but I was convinced by *The Screwtape Letters* that it was important to attend the local parish, rather than the parish that one likes.[4] Church is not a social club. So I swallowed my personal preferences and attended the more contemporary liturgy of my local parish. On one of my first Sundays there, I noticed a beautiful violinist among the musicians, and my immediate thought was, "No, she is too pretty not to have a boyfriend. And you need to focus on your prayers."

I had much the same feeling when it came to both Durham and All Saints: "I am not cool enough to be here." From a young age, I was stodgy to the point of curmudgeonliness,

[4] C. S. Lewis, *The Screwtape Letters* (New York: HarperOne, 1942), letter 16.

and the years have not made me younger. My uniform at the time was a gray or brown sweater over a shirt and tie, with khakis. I wore round, Dietrich Bonhoeffer glasses that were constantly mistaken for Harry Potter glasses. And although I was eager to fit in by making sure people knew that I did not think homosexual acts were more heinous sins than my own vainglory, I was at heart a traditionalist. My socialism was slowly fading into Chestertonian distributism, by which the goal is not collective control of all productive property but the widest possible distribution of it. Thanks to another professor, Dr. Grillo, I had a growing love of Wendell Berry with all his traditional, agrarian values. Meanwhile, both the parish and the town were cool, and I felt that I stuck out like a sore thumb.

The Anglican Episcopal House of Studies at Duke Divinity is its seminary program, and I made an effort to frequent its Morning Prayer service. One day a week, the Office was sung, giving me my first experience of the English tradition of Gregorian chant and of semimonastic prayer in something like the form in which it was originally intended. But it was not frequent enough for me to get really accustomed to it, and though I appreciated it in theory, I was trying too hard to follow along with a musical tradition I did not understand to appreciate properly what was a truly beautiful and divine service.

It was Duke that finally broke me of my socialist affiliation and my compromises with liberalism. I had already disagreed with many of their positions and insisted on moderating their views on economics. I did not change my actual intellectual position much, but I underwent a change of disposition. What I saw was not a fault in an argument that I had not seen before but the reality of the Left's endgame, and I found it almost physically repulsive. An extremism existed at Duke, especially in the seminary, which had not yet reached Baylor's mainstream liberals—at

Duke there was an insistence on twisting and breaking the thing I held most dear: the tradition. I recoiled and was happy to retreat to the Religion Department, where most of the liberals I interacted with belonged to an older school of more classical liberalism, one with which I felt I could disagree reasonably, whereas this other progressive Left made me feel a need to gird myself for war.

As I began to encounter the wider Anglican world outside the Diocese of Fort Worth, it became clear that the catholicity of this tradition was less sure than I had thought. I distinctly remember a conversation in which the rector of All Saints said that "most Anglicans" would call the Presence of Christ in the Eucharist "a moral presence". That was shocking to me, as my theology of Communion came entirely from the Fathers and Pope Benedict. I could not imagine that our tradition's predominant view of the Real Presence could be so impoverished. By this time, I was familiar with Flannery O'Connor's famous reaction to this view: "If it is just a symbol, then to hell with it." It was clear to me that this "moral" presence was little better. I stood by the words of John 6:55, η γαρ σαρξ μου αληθως βρωμις: "For my flesh is food indeed."

I was also deeply disappointed that our communion was more interested in seeking fellowship with a Messianic Jewish denomination than with the Polish Old Catholics or the Eastern Orthodox—or with the conservative Lutherans of the Missouri Synod. That felt like an almost personal betrayal. The subject of Church unity was growing in importance to me, with a focus on Christ's high priestly prayer in John 17:11, "That they may be one", and John Henry Newman's Tract 11 from the *Tracts for the Times*, on the visible nature of the Church.[5] These texts,

[5] John Henry Newman, "The Visible Church", Tract 11, *Tracts for the Times*, http://anglicanhistory.org/tracts/tract11.html.

along with texts such as Ephesians 3, make clear the imperative need for a visible unity in the Church, one of real, concrete fellowship, not the unity of Luther's "invisible Church", which neither Newman nor I could find anywhere in Scripture. The more I encountered Anglicans, the more I felt this was not what I had signed up for.

I began to have a sneaking suspicion that I had joined the wrong church for my views. The Anglican churches were unable to resolve even basic disagreements about the ordination of women, giving me flashbacks to the inability of Messianics to settle basic disagreements about calendars and kosher food. As a result, members of traditional jurisdictions who did not believe it was possible to ordain women to the priesthood were not able to take Communion in some jurisdictions of their own denomination. Endless committees were commissioned, but no one was convinced by opposing arguments, no one changed his mind, and no solution was seriously proposed, let alone implemented. The church was barely in communion with itself, let alone with anyone else! While the Anglican Church in North America stayed together, they struggled to share clergy due to these differences, and often it was necessary for communicants of this denomination, when visiting another diocese, to go outside their own denomination—either to a different Anglican church not in their communion or even to a Lutheran church—in order to have Communion with clergy whom they recognized as such.

By the end of my first semester, the fall of 2013, I had learned that the violinist at church was, in fact, single. Her name was Carrie, and I was screwing up the nerve to ask her on a date, which I would do at a Super Bowl party hosted by one of our parish's seminarians. She eventually said yes, and shortly after, we began dating.

At the same time, I decided I needed to find out why Newman, who was the reason I became an Anglican, had left for Catholicism. I picked up *An Essay on the Development of Christian Doctrine*. I also began reading Pope Benedict's *Many Religions—One Covenant*, which resolved many of my lingering issues about the relationship of the Church to Israel. He writes:

> This view of a deep unity between the good news of Jesus and the message of Sinai is again summarized in the reference to a statement of the New Testament . . . : the whole Law, including the Prophets, depends on the twofold yet one commandment of love of God and love of neighbor. . . . For the nations, being assumed into the children of Abraham is concretely realized in entering into the will of God in which moral commandment and profession of the oneness of God are indivisible, as this becomes clear especially in Saint Mark's version of this tradition, in which the double commandment is expressly linked to the "Shema Israel", to the Yes to the one and only God. Man's way is prescribed for him; he is to measure himself according to the standard of God and according to his own human perfection.[6]

According to him, Christ's mission was to "unite Jews and pagans into a single People of God in which the universalist promises of the Scriptures are fulfilled",[7] referring especially to the promises of Isaiah that the Gentiles would be included. But all this is "without the abolishment of the special mission of Israel".[8] But in order to incorporate the Gentiles as true sons of Abraham, by adoption through Christ, the particularity of the Law of Moses—directed, as it was, to a specific people in a specific land—had to be "broadened", in Ratzinger's terms, not liberalized, as a

[6] Joseph Ratzinger, *Many Religions—One Covenant: Israel, the Church, and the World*, trans. Graham Harrison (San Francisco: Ignatius Press, 1999), 33–34.

[7] Ibid., 26.

[8] Ibid., 27.

progressive reformer would have it; the depths of its intentions had to be brought to the surface so that they could be fully applied to the whole world.[9] This is what Christ does in the Sermon on the Mount with His series of "You have heard that it was said, but I say to you" juxtapositions.

Much as when I read Chesterton's *Orthodoxy*, I felt that Newman was clearly more likely to be right than I was, but I was still hesitant to commit myself to the Catholic Church. Newman spoke to my heart when he wrote:

> It is in point to notice also the structure and style of Scripture, a structure so unsystematic and various, and a style so figurative and indirect, that no one would presume at first sight to say what is in it and what is not. It cannot, as it were, be mapped, or its contents catalogued; but after all our diligence, to the end of our lives and to the end of the Church, it must be an unexplored and unsubdued land, with heights and valleys, forests and streams, on the right and left of our path and close about us, full of concealed wonders and choice treasures. Of no doctrine whatever, which does not actually contradict what has been delivered, can it be peremptorily asserted that it is not in Scripture; of no reader, whatever be his study of it, can it be said that he has mastered every doctrine which it contains.[10]

This was, in principle, the same thing that had so clearly impressed itself on me five years before: that the Bible is complex and multiform and does not give even necessary answers to important practical questions—questions, in fact, that are theological and ethical and appear to be within its proper realm. It is not perspicuous; it is not self-interpreting, at least not entirely; and it requires some

[9] Ibid., 38–41.

[10] John Henry Newman, *An Essay on the Development of Christian Doctrine*, 6th ed. (Notre Dame, Ind.: University of Notre Dame Press, 1989), 71.

kind of normalizing authority from outside itself to give context and authorize right interpretation. But Newman did not stop there; he pressed on to the problem that had plagued me even longer, for seven years, since we first visited Beit HaDerekh:

> There can be no combination on the basis of truth without an organ of truth. As cultivation brings out the colours of flowers, and domestication changes the character of animals, so does education of necessity develope differences of opinion; and while it is impossible to lay down first principles in which all will unite, it is utterly unreasonable to expect that this man should yield to that, or all to one. I do not say there are no eternal truths ... which all acknowledge in private, but that there are none sufficiently commanding to be the basis of public union and action. The only general persuasive in matters of conduct is authority; that is, (when truth is in question,) a judgment which we feel to be superior to our own. If Christianity is both social and dogmatic, and intended for all ages, it must humanly speaking have an infallible expounder. Else you will secure unity of form at the loss of unity of doctrine, or unity of doctrine at the loss of unity of form; you will have to choose between a comprehension of opinions and a resolution into parties.[11]

Without some recognized authority, unity was impossible, because on what grounds did a person recognize one view, developed by a reasonable person out of reasonable though inherently incomplete information, over another that was formulated in the same way? And how can a person ask the holder of one opinion to submit to the other? If Christ meant what He prayed at the Last Supper, "that they may be one" (Jn 17:11), why would He then leave a

[11] Ibid., 90.

Church hopelessly incapable of achieving that unity, without the essential implements of it?

I can give no good reason why I did not convert on the spot. I maintained that the Tradition of the Church and the apostolic succession, broadly speaking, were still sufficient to meet that need, despite mounting evidence. Over the next year or so, the hollowness of the unity that the Anglican Communion preserved would become abundantly clear as it prepared to abandon that hollow unity for "a resolution into parties". Neither of the options was acceptable, but I thought the choice of hollow unity was preferable to the dissolution into parties. Of course, I may have been a little preoccupied in the spring of 2014. I was in love with a beautiful girl and things were going well, and my theological problems were put on hold.

I knew almost nothing about books of hours or diurnals or the Roman Rite, but I began on occasion to divert my daily prayer habit from the BCP's Daily Office to a simple rite made up only of psalms for Lauds and Vespers each day, together with the Kyrie and the Our Father, and concluding with a Hail Mary. This change was inspired not only by my love of psalms but by my reading Paul Bradshaw's historical survey *Early Christian Worship*, especially his description of the early Cathedral Office, the mother of the later Roman and Benedictine Liturgies of the Hours. Bradshaw highlighted the continuity of this practice with the Jewish tradition of daily prayer from which it sprang and its connection in the second and third centuries with the instruction in 1 Thessalonians to "pray constantly", a connection I had long maintained.[12] This endless liturgy is the way we offer our perpetual sacrifice of praise, the Christian daily sacrifice. Bradshaw writes:

[12] Paul F. Bradshaw, *Early Christian Worship: A Basic Introduction to Ideas and Practice*, 2nd ed. (Collegeville, Minn.: Liturgical Press, 2010), 77–80.

> Psalms 148–150 seem to have formed the nucleus of the morning praise everywhere, together with the canticle *Gloria in Excelsis* in the East. The evening seems to have been less fixed, but the hymn *Phos hilaron*, "Hail gladdening light," was often used in the East as the lamps were lit and thanksgiving offered for the natural light of the day, for the lamplight in the darkness of the night, and for the illumination brought by the light of Christ. Psalm 63, understood to refer to morning, and Psalm 141 with its reference to evening are also found at those hours in many Eastern rites.[13]

This passage is heavily underlined in my copy of *Early Christian Worship*. Though it overlapped only somewhat with my early instincts, the coincidence of Psalm 141 in the Evening Office had me elated. I had been right all along! The short, simple Office, made up almost entirely of psalms and the Our Father, was the ancient Daily Office. I remember reading this by yellow lamplight at night in my little study, in the apartment I had nicknamed the Hermitage of the Southern March in homage to C. S. Lewis. A mystic triumph to the sound of *Phos hilaron* echoed in my ears.

A strange transition began to overtake me. The language of the BCP began to feel stale and stifling, dry as ash in my mouth. The only parts I still enjoyed were the texts of Scripture and the Creed. The collects and prefaces were pale and bloodless in comparison with the psalm-heavy Cathedral Office. The concerns of the prayers were sterile and academic in comparison to the cris de coeur that were the requests of the psalmists. I still loved the book, but I felt very much that it was being torn away from me and overwhelmed by the magnificence of my first love: the Psalter itself as prayer book.

[13] Ibid., 80.

There can be no question that the first of these two prayers, lovely in its own way, pales in comparison to the second:

> Almighty and most merciful Father,
> we have erred and strayed from thy ways like lost sheep,
> we have followed too much the devices and desires of our own hearts,
> we have offended against thy holy laws,
> we have left undone those things which we ought to have done,
> and we have done those things which we ought not to have done.
> But thou, O Lord, have mercy upon us,
> spare thou those who confess their faults,
> restore thou those who are penitent,
> according to thy promises declared unto mankind
> in Christ Jesus our Lord;
> and grant, O most merciful Father, for his sake,
> that we may hereafter live a godly, righteous, and sober life,
> to the glory of thy holy Name. Amen.[14]

> Have mercy upon me, O God, according to thy lovingkindness: according unto the multitude of thy tender mercies blot out my transgressions.
> Wash me thoroughly from mine iniquity, and cleanse me from my sin.
> For I acknowledge my transgressions: and my sin is ever before me....
> Behold, I was shapen in iniquity; and in sin did my mother conceive me....

[14] Episcopal Church, *The Book of Common Prayer and Administration of the Sacraments and Other Rites and Ceremonies of the Church: Together with the Psalter or Psalms of David According to the Use of the Episcopal Church* (New York: Seabury Press, 1979), 41–42.

> Purge me with hyssop, and I shall be clean: wash
> me, and I shall be whiter than snow.
> Make me to hear joy and gladness; that the bones
> which thou hast broken may rejoice.
> Hide thy face from my sins, and blot out all mine
> iniquities.
> Create in me a clean heart, O God; and renew a
> right spirit within me. . . .
> Restore unto me the joy of thy salvation; and
> uphold me with thy free spirit.
> Then will I teach transgressors thy ways; and
> sinners shall be converted unto thee.
> (Ps 51:1–3, 5, 7–10, 12–13, KJV)

At this time, I began to think about and talk to some friends about a project to translate the Psalms poetically—not merely metrically but really taking into account their native principles of verse and prosody. I spoke to an artist and a musician and a couple of poets about the idea of creating a new translation of the Psalter on poetic principles, with an eye to chant, and illustrated in the form of medieval illuminations. I wanted it to be a book that took seriously the idea that the Psalms are the hymnal of the Bible. It was a passion project, and I sank many hours into it. This project stalled while I was working on my Ph.D. because I lacked time to pursue it, but I remain proud of what we achieved, the best work being done by our poet and our illustrator.

15

In June 2014, Carrie and I visited a parish belonging to another Anglican splinter group of a very High Church nature, the Anglican Catholic Church, for a midweek service. The liturgy was refreshing after the very Evangelical atmosphere of our parish, and it introduced me to the 1928 Book of Common Prayer, but the language was still too dry for me after the stiff dram of the Cathedral Office. It also encouraged my interest in learning about the situation of our communion and its splinter groups, a subject that was extremely disheartening. In 2014, the Anglican Communion was in the process of tearing itself apart over the liberalization of its wealthiest members—the United Kingdom, Ireland, Canada, America, and New Zealand in particular. Some fifty years before, a smaller number of parishes and bishops had left the Episcopal Church in the United States over the ordination of women and the revision of the prayer book. The Anglican Catholic Church was one of several fractured communions that emerged from that earlier split.

A few disturbing trends stood out to me. Although in the United States, the Anglican Church in North America (ACNA) had separated from the Episcopal Church, the ACNA was recognized as a full member of the communion by the large churches in the Global South, with particularly strong ties to the churches in Chile, Argentina, Rwanda, Uganda, Jerusalem, and the Middle East. The archbishop of Canterbury delayed for a very long time making any specific movement or statement on the issue but finally made clear that he did not consider the ACNA to be a member church of the Anglican Communion.[1] As a result, the Global South churches, almost without exception, amended their constitutions to exclude "communion with the Archbishop of Canterbury" as a sign of a true Anglican church. This was a clear precursor to schism, and it filled me with dread. It suggested that we were prepared to take the atomistic course over hollow unity, but I was resistant. After all, once we admit the legitimacy of schism in principle, on what grounds do we draw the line anywhere? The ACNA itself was tearing at the seams over the ordination of women, and I could not see on what principle we could say that it needed to stay together rather than splitting into an anti-women's-ordination faction aligned with the Church of Nigeria and a pro-ordination faction aligned with the Church of Kenya.

The distinction between the excommunication that led to the Great Schism and the "church splits" that led to the breakup of the Anglican Communion were put into sharp contrast. It is one thing to tell a heretic that he is a heretic and not welcome at the table of the Lord until he repents, as Saint Paul warns in 1 Corinthians 11:27–34. It is another entirely to say, "Our church is no longer part of that church." Those are different claims about the nature of the Church, and it underscores the problems that Newman identified with the idea of an invisible Church. If there is any unity, it must be the visible unity of the visible Church.

[1] In February 2023, the Church of England voted to bless homosexual "marriages", with the result that the Global South Fellowship of Anglican Churches, including all those mentioned above, as well as the largest branch of the communion, the Church of Nigeria, no longer recognize the archbishop of Canterbury as the leader of the Anglican Communion and are no longer in communion with the Church of England and other liberal churches.

As Anglicans, we liked to quote Lutheran theologian Rupertus Meldenius' principle, "In essentials unity, in nonessentials liberty, and in all things charity", but this was not really an actionable principle. On what grounds or by what authority could we distinguish between essentials and nonessentials? If we accepted no authority's conclusions on matters of doctrine, whose conclusions would we accept on which doctrines were essential? It was abundantly clear that not only could we not agree on the ordination of women, but we could also not even agree on whether it was an essential. What is worse, the Anglican conferences and councils operated by majority vote! And though democracy may be a desirable means for governing nations, we must agree that it is a terrible system for discerning truth. Without a visible source of unity endowed with authority from on high, I could adduce no principle for discerning essentials nor for enforcing a view on any of them, as Newman had so clearly argued in his *Essay*. I was right back where I started as a Messianic.

Lest this sound like a form of special pleading, and that churches do not actually split over petty nonsense, let me offer an example. A few years after this, while I was in Scotland, I learned that the Free Church of Scotland—that is, the conservative offshoot of the Church of Scotland—was in the midst of a split over whether it was permissible to sing any hymns other than the psalms in church. I explained this to a friend and colleague from the Netherlands who was training to be a Dutch Reformed pastor. He laughed out loud and told me, "Our conservative branch already concluded that you can't sing anything other than the psalms, and they are now in the midst of a split over whether it is permissible to use new melodies for singing them!" Once church schism is accepted in principle, there is truly no bottom.

At the same time, I was becoming deeply interested in the Celtic church of the early medieval period. Thankfully, the Celtic Romanticism of the 1990s had passed by and a more Catholic understanding of the early Christian communities of Ireland and Scotland had prevailed. These were fascinating communities of extreme dedication to prayer and penance. This fascination rescued me from falling into a fallacy that was raised to defend the legitimacy of the Anglican Communion: the idea of the independent Celtic church. Even a cursory reading of the life of Saint Columbanus and his letters would serve to dispel the idea that the Celts did not recognize the universal jurisdiction of the pope,[2] but the claim originally made by the Celtic Romantics has never fully gone away. In fact, for me, hearing that argument undermined Anglicanism's claims to antiquity. Which Celtic distinctives did Anglicanism preserve? Its Latin liturgy, or the Bangor Antiphonary? Its archiepiscopal sees? Its dating of Easter? Its monastic tradition? Its proclivity for semi-Pelagianism? No! Quite the opposite in every single case. Our liturgy was vernacular and derived from the Roman use; our archiepiscopal sees were based on the later Roman mission to the Anglo-Saxons, not the primitive Celtic church. We dated Easter with the rest of the Latin world, and our proclivity was toward extreme Calvinism as an error, rather than the works-righteousness error of Pelagius. Nothing about our church was remotely Celtic, and the Celts recognized the primacy of the Holy See!

On September 8, 2014, I asked Carrie to marry me after asking her father's blessing over Labor Day weekend. I took her to dinner while a friend strewed my living

[2] See George Metlake, *The Life and Writings of St. Columban* (Whitefish, Mont.: Literary Licensing, 1914).

room with rose petals and set out candles and champagne. When we entered the room, I picked up a claddagh ring, knelt, and asked her if she would marry me. We began planning a wedding for January, a date chosen for us by the due dates of a nephew on one side of the family and a niece on the other.

Shortly thereafter, I wrote a blog entry on the vital need for a better love for and theology of the Blessed Virgin Mary, especially for the sake of our ecclesiology that she is the image of the Church and our model. I also explained that she is the model for us of both virginity and fertility and that she is the essential piece for us in the cultural debates over gender, sex, and virginity. But my main concern was her role in ecclesiology as the mystic Bride, tied to what I had learned as a Messianic about our essentially feminine role with respect to Christ, our Bridegroom. I was desperate for this high ecclesiology because I saw my own communion falling apart around me, denying Christ's plea for our unity. The Blessed Virgin defines the feminine for us, and her inner singleness of will defines the unity of the Church. Carrie and I found a white porcelain statue of Mary, tall and slender. We placed it on our home oratory—our mother, our model, a shining light of virginal purity—and it quickly became a focal point of my meditation.[3]

On January 24, 2015, Carrie and I were married according to the rites of the Anglican church in St. Mary's chapel, a little nineteenth-century red brick Gothic Revival building that stands on a low rise beside a gently sloping pasture beneath the North Carolina pines, far from the noise of the city. After we made our vows, the priest celebrated

[3] The statue has since been broken by a rambunctious toddler, but we are looking for a replacement.

Communion according to the provisional Texts for Common Prayer of 2013 from the Anglican Church in North America. The altar was wooden, bolted to the east wall, and I considered it a small triumph over Evangelicalism that the priest was forced by default to celebrate *ad orientem*, much to his chagrin. The church was almost Cistercian in simplicity, all clear glass and sunlight on whitewashed walls and creaking wooden floors and wooden pews. The minister's wife accompanied the ceremony on her harp. Communion received, we adjourned to a hall in Chapel Hill, where we had contra dancing and Carolina barbecue was catered.

In April, I wrote a blog entry titled "The Untamed Wilderness" on the primacy of Tradition over Scripture on the grounds of Newman's analogy for the nature of Scripture. I pointed out that the apostolic churches were, in fact, more unified in creedal and Christological dogma than they were in the content of the canon of Scripture. In fact, in 1994, Pope John Paul II and the patriarch of the Church of the East—a church that does not accept the books of 2 Peter, 2 and 3 John, Jude, and Revelation and that separated from the Catholic Church after the Council of Ephesus in A.D. 431, making it the oldest standing schism in the Church—signed a joint Christological statement. This statement affirmed not only the doctrine of the later Council of Chalcedon (A.D. 451) about the nature of Christ but also the Symbol of Athanasius, the great statement of Catholic orthodoxy on Christ's divine-human nature!

Even the churches that do not affirm the Council of Chalcedon, which defined the nature of Christ, are more akin to Catholic Christianity on the nature of Christ than on the books of the Bible. And that, even without the complex and paradoxical nature of Scripture itself, bears witness that the Tradition was the basis of the Church, her life, her teaching, and her unity. It was clear that this was a death knell. I was now attending the Anglican church on Sunday mornings and often sneaking away to Mass on weekdays and Saturday or Sunday evenings.

The last time I ever attended our Anglican parish, the priest who had married Carrie and me used a different liturgy than usual. It was from one of the East African churches and was mostly unobjectionable, except when it came to the Eucharistic Prayer. Like the 1662 Book of Common Prayer, but unlike those with which I was familiar—the 1928, the 1979, and ACNA's own Texts for Common Prayer—it contained no form of Epiclesis, no appeal to the Holy Spirit to bless the bread and wine. In contrast with the East, the Western version of this prayer is traditionally very short, appearing in the Roman Eucharistic Rite II as "Make holy, therefore, these gifts, we pray, by sending down your Spirit upon them like the dewfall, so that they may become for us the Body and Blood of our Lord Jesus Christ."[4]

This, to me, implied a radically different doctrine of Communion and of what was happening on the altar. If we did not need the Holy Spirit to change the elements, then they were a mere memorial, and why on earth were we bothering? In the words of Flannery O'Connor, "To hell with it." I refused to receive Communion, and I never went back. I went straight to the nearest Catholic parish and inquired about RCIA classes.

[4] *The Roman Missal* (Totowa, N.J.: Catholic Book Publishing Corp., 2011), 498.

Part V

The Jerusalem Above (2015–Present)

16

When I left All Saints for the last time in the late summer or early fall of 2015, I was already convinced of the truth of the Catholic faith in its entirety. For me, going through RCIA was a formality. I had acquired a *Catechism of the Catholic Church* at a secondhand bookshop and frequently referred to it. But now I was married, and, like Chesterton, I wanted to enter the Church with my wife.

Scheduling RCIA classes became a complicated problem, and we were not able to begin until January 2016. I had graduated with an M.A. from Duke in the spring of 2015 and had been accepted to the Ph.D. program in Hebrew Bible and Old Testament at the University of St Andrews, though I had to delay matriculating there for a year, until the fall of 2016. In the meantime, I was working as a "preceptor", a kind of teaching assistant much like the tutors of the British University tradition, at Duke Divinity School. Carrie and I had a wonderful catechist who taught us privately due to our scheduling problems, through the Catholic Student Center at Duke. But we were not able to complete the course before the Paschal season. Much of this time, Carrie was still attending All Saints and then coming to Mass with me afterward. It was a community in which she was invested, playing music and teaching students, and she was hesitant just to abandon it because of objections I had that she did not share.

We left Durham and spent that summer going back and forth between my family in Texas and Carrie's in

Connecticut in preparation for our big adventure to Scotland. In Midland, we attended my parents' Anglican parish, and I also went to Mass at a nearby Catholic parish. The last day we were in town, I had a sudden and almost oppressive desire: I needed to buy a copy of the Rule of Saint Benedict. This turned out to be rather a tall order. After driving to every bookstore in town, I found a single copy in the back of Our Lady of Guadalupe's little bookshop, a predominantly Spanish-language shop for a predominantly Spanish-speaking parish and convent. The book was a paraphrase in an odd, blue faux-leather cover, but I devoured it. In the Hours as Saint Benedict described them, I found the liturgy I had been looking for ever since I was in high school: it was predominantly psalms, and it used all of them. It had been right here all along: the biblical liturgy that I tried to create in a trailer home in Tzafririm had been created fourteen hundred years earlier by Saint Benedict in a cave in Subiaco. My breast felt like a flower blossoming in the spring, opening out at the miracle of the thing I had been seeking for ten years, since my first dabbling with daily prayer.

I had a little King James Psalter, and on the back of a prayer card with an image of *Christ Pantocrator*, Christ the Ruler of All, I wrote out the order of psalms for Lauds and Vespers (Morning and Evening Prayer) for each day of the week. I used the card as a bookmark, and this became my prayer book. I did not learn the hymns, lessons, responses, and Collects until later. This, to me, was prayer in its purest form—the true prayer book, the ancient Siddur, the Temple's hymnal, and the liturgy of Christ Himself.

On our way out of town, I complained to Carrie about the substitution of a lame modern praise song for the Gloria, which, though technically allowed in the rubrics of the BCP, I argued is almost always a bad idea. The Gloria is both one of our most ancient and beautiful hymns and also practically the Creed in the form of praise. Carrie interrupted my rant to say, "Why don't you write that? That's interesting. It's the kind of thing people actually want to know about."

So I paradoxically began a series of articles on the Book of Common Prayer and its rubrics when I was already convinced of the Catholic faith and was in the process of converting. The *North American Anglican* picked up the first three or four installments of this series—all that I ever actually wrote. My finest ode to the Anglicanism that I loved was my elegy to it when it had become an artwork to admire rather than a faith to believe.

When we arrived in St Andrews, we very quickly began attending the little Catholic parish of St James on a cliff above the North Sea, joined the choir, and enrolled once again in the RCIA program. As in Durham, though, scheduling conflicts remained. Much of Carrie's work as a private violin teacher has always been in the evenings, when things like RCIA classes are typically scheduled. The parish priest, Father Michael John, agreed that if I would talk to her about what I had learned in the classes, it would suffice for her catechesis. In reality, her catechesis came from reading about three-quarters of the *Catechism of the Catholic Church* straight through. The experience was eye-opening for her. Things that had required a great deal of explanation in her Reformed Protestantism were clarified and made a great deal more sense in the teaching of the Catholic Church. Before the spring semester came, Carrie was fully convinced of the truth of Catholicism as well.

Carrie's conversion was certainly not harmed by the fact that the Catholic chaplaincy was rife with future saints. All the students we met were admirable young people, and not a few of them were of outstanding virtue. The one who stands out to me most was Ben, now Brother Edmund at Pluscarden Abbey, a young man of extraordinary devotion who did me the baffling honor of asking my advice on questions of both theology and devotion, when it was obvious to me that I should have been the one asking him. I distinctly remember discussing the hours of prayer with him on a fine, warm spring afternoon in the courtyard of St Mary's College, with the great gray King James Library at our backs and the sun in our faces.

Carrie and I spent a great deal of time in and around the chaplaincy, directly across the street from the parish. On the second floor was a plain little chapel for the students whose north-facing windows looked out over the North Sea coast of Fife, as far as Dundee and the rolling green hills of Angus. I listened to Peter Kreeft's moving lecture on the sea and thought of that view of the West Sands and the mouth of the River Tay, where the waves steadily and gently roll upon the beach just below the Old Course.

We were received into full communion with the one, holy, catholic, and apostolic Church at the Easter Vigil in May 2017 in the parish church of St James. I chose Saint Jerome as my patron, and Carrie chose Saint Thérèse of Lisieux. I cannot say that I had the oft-heard converts' story of the heavens opening upon their first reception of the true Eucharist. Perhaps I was too familiar with the dogma for too long to experience it afresh. When the heavens did not open, I remember thinking, "It's what Rich said: 'This is what liturgy offers that all the razzmatazz of our modern worship can't touch. You don't go home from church going, "Oh I am just moved to tears." You go home from church going, "Wow, I just took communion and you know what? If Augustine were alive today, he would have had it with me and maybe he is and maybe he did."'"[5] But

[5]Jimmy Abegg, "Jimmy Abegg—Reflections of Rich", *CCM Magazine*, September 15, 2017, www.ccmmagazine.com/features/jimmy-abegg-reflections-of-rich.

the change that came over me was remarkable and perhaps more in keeping with my own history and personal calling: I can honestly say that I went the rest of the spring and the whole summer without mortal sin—a feat I had never accomplished before and have not repeated since, and a clear sign of divine intervention in my frail will.

Unbeknownst to Carrie and me until a week or so before we were confirmed, a friend from Duke and one of my fellow workers on the Psalter project, Evan, was received the same day, several time zones away in Indiana. A little over a year later, our firstborn, Wendell Nicholas Wiseman, was born in the hospital in Dundee. He was baptized in the same church where we were received into the Catholic Church. We named Evan his godfather, and his godmother, Katy, was Carrie's Confirmation sponsor and a fellow Anglican convert.

17

Since becoming Catholic, I have continued to work out my understanding of how to interpret Scripture and the role and authority of the Church in doing so. A major step came in the library at St Andrews when I stumbled upon a book titled *Literature as Communication* by Roger Sell. His thesis is that literature is not categorically different from ordinary conversation in how it functions and conveys meaning. To most of us, this sounds intuitive, but it is controversial in academia.

The fact that literature works in more or less the same way as conversation comes with several important implications. Conversations always take place in a context of time, place, culture, and personality. These factors are no less a part of a book than the words of the book themselves. This is the main problem for readers: How do you understand a book that was written by someone in a wildly different context from your own? Sell's theory is that you need a "mediating critic", someone who can introduce you to the context of the work and the life of the author. Sell particularly recommends literary biography because it introduces readers to both the general historical context and the individual author, who may have been odd or had unusual views in his time.

Sell's book struck me like a revelation. He was saying the same thing Newman had said about the Bible, but he worked it out in much more detail. Newman's insistence that Scripture cannot be self-interpreting and requires some unifying authority with final, clarifying say over controversies was put in a new light by Sell and his theory of mediating criticism. What I found particularly compelling about this comparison is the fact that the Church very rarely gives one definitive interpretation of a text of Scripture that must be accepted. That happens only in specific cases of controversy over major theological points. The rest of the time, the Church seems to provide a general interpretive context for Scripture, much like Sell's notion.

I discovered Sell's book in the summer of 2017, soon after being received into the Church, and much of my work since has revolved around applying it to the Catholic interpretation of Scripture. We believe, in accordance with the Fathers and Doctors of the Church, that Scripture has two authors: the Divine Author and the human author. But if God is the Author of Scripture, how can we as limited, fallible, sinful human beings possibly understand the authorial context enough to interpret His book properly?

The answer is that God has provided a spiritual mediating critic by giving His Spirit to the Church, particularly her bishops, to "guide [her] into all the truth" (Jn 16:13). Through Baptism and Holy Communion, the Incarnate Christ has joined Himself to His Church. The Body of Christ is the eternal, ongoing mediating critic and, at the same time, is itself the divine context of the Bible, principally through the successors of the apostles, to whom Jesus promised the Spirit. And at their head sit Peter and His successors, the bishops of Rome, who have the final, clarifying say in matters of controversy.

Previously, my study of the Bible and how it is interpreted constantly led to new obstacles and complete revisions of my approach. Now there are new puzzles, but the solution to each puzzle points clearly along the same course I have already taken. The Bible as a whole makes sense to me now, and the further I pursue my research, the more clearly I understand it and how to interpret it. I have continued to pursue this line of thinking since Carrie and I moved back to the United States in 2019 and am preparing journal articles and two books to explain it in more depth. Since moving back, we have had two more children, Bennett and Lucy. After six years in the Catholic Church, I have no regrets, and while I continue to have puzzles and questions, I have no doubt that this is home. This is where I belong.

RECOMMENDED READING

Benedict XVI, Pope. *Jesus of Nazareth: From the Baptism in the Jordan to the Transfiguration*. Translated by Adrian J. Walker. San Francisco: Ignatius Press, 2008.

———. *Jesus of Nazareth: Holy Week from the Entrance into Jerusalem to the Resurrection*. Translation provided by the Vatican Secretariat of State. San Francisco: Ignatius Press, 2023.

———. *Jesus of Nazareth: The Infancy Narratives*. Translated by Philip J. Whitmore. New York: Image Books, 2012.

———. *Many Religions—One Covenant: Israel, the Church, and the World*. Translated by Graham Harrison. San Francisco: Ignatius Press, 1999.

Bennett, Rod. *Four Witnesses: The Early Church in Her Own Words*. San Francisco: Ignatius Press, 2002.

Bradshaw, Paul F. *Early Christian Worship: A Basic Introduction to Ideas and Practice*. Collegeville, Minn.: Liturgical Press, 2010.

Catechism of the Catholic Church. 2nd ed. Città del Vaticano: Libreria Editrice Vaticana, 1997.

Chesterton, G.K. *The Everlasting Man*. San Francisco: Ignatius Press, 1993. First published 1925.

———. *Orthodoxy: The Romance of Faith*. Peabody, Ma.: Hendrickson Publishers, 2006. First published 1908.

Farkasfalvy, Denis. *Inspiration and Interpretation: A Theological Introduction to Sacred Scripture*. Washington, D.C.: Catholic University of America Press, 2010.

Hahn, Scott. *The Lamb's Supper: The Mass as Heaven on Earth*. New York: Doubleday, 1999.

Hooker, Morna D. *The Gospel according to Saint Mark*, Black's New Testament Commentary. Peabody, Ma.: Hendrickson Publishers, 2009.

Jeffrey, David Lyle. *People of the Book: Christian Identity and Literary Culture*. Grand Rapids, Mich.: William B. Eerdmans with the Institute for Advanced Christian Studies, 1996.

Jones, Cheslyn, Geoffrey Wainwright, Edward Yarnold, and Paul Bradshaw, eds. *The Study of Liturgy*. Rev. ed. London: SPCK, 1992.

Justin Martyr. *Dialogue with Trypho*. Washington, D.C.: Catholic University of America Press, 2003.

Kreeft, Peter. *Summa of the Summa*. San Francisco: Ignatius Press, 1990.

Kugel, James L. *How to Read the Bible: A Guide to Scripture, Then and Now*. New York: Free Press, 2007.

Newman, John Henry. *Apologia Pro Vita Sua: Being a History of His Religious Opinions*. Oxford, UK: Oxford University Press, 1967.

———. *An Essay on the Development of Christian Doctrine*. Notre Dame, Ind.: University of Notre Dame Press, 1994.

Sparks, Kenton L. *Ancient Texts for the Study of the Hebrew Bible: A Guide to the Background Literature*. Peabody, Ma.: Hendrickson Publishers, 2005.